Multicultural
Counseling
Competencies

MULTICULTURAL ASPECTS OF COUNSELING SERIES

SERIES EDITOR
Paul Pedersen, Ph.D., *University of Alabama at Birmingham*

EDITORIAL BOARD

VOLUMES IN THIS SERIES

Multicultural Counseling Competencies

Individual and Organizational Development

Derald Wing Sue
Robert T. Carter
J. Manuel Casas
Nadya A. Fouad
Allen E. Ivey
Margaret Jensen
Teresa LaFromboise
Jeanne E. Manese
Joseph G. Ponterotto
Ena Vazquez-Nutall

Multicultural Aspects of Counseling Series 11

SAGE Publications
International Educational and Professional Publisher
Thousand Oaks   London   New Delhi

For information:

SAGE Publications, Inc.
2455 Teller Road
Thousand Oaks, California 91320
E-mail: order@sagepub.com

SAGE Publications Ltd.
6 Bonhill Street
London EC2A 4PU
United Kingdom

SAGE Publications India Pvt. Ltd.
M-32 Market
Greater Kailash I
New Delhi 110 048 India

Printed in the United States of America

Library of Congress Cataloging-in-Publication Data

Main entry under title:
    Multicultural counseling competencies: individual and organizational
development / by Derald Wing Sue . . . [et al.].
      p. cm. — (Multicultural aspects of counseling; v. 11)
    Includes bibliographical references and index.
    ISBN 0-8039-7130-3 (cloth: alk. paper). — ISBN 0-8039-7131-1 (pbk.: alk. paper)
    1. Cross-cultural counseling—United States. 2. Multiculturalism—
United States. 3. Counselors—Training of—United States.
I. Sue, Derald Wing. II. Series.
BF637.C6M837 1998
158'.3—dc21   97-45323

This book is printed on acid-free paper.

98 99 00 01 02 03 10 9 8 7 6 5 4 3 2 1

Acquiring Editor:	Jim Nageotte
Editorial Assistant:	Fiona Lyon
Production Editor:	Sherrise M. Purdum
Production Assistant:	Denise Santoyo
Typesetter:	Rebecca Evans
Indexer:	Teri Greenberg
Print Buyer:	Anna Chin

Contents

Foreword

The implications of defined multicultural competencies are profound for the profession of counseling. First, now that these competencies have been defined and accepted by the American Counseling Association and both Divisions 17 and 45 of the American Psychological Association, they need to be central components of counseling programs rather than an adjunct to training. Second, practicing counselors are legally vulnerable when they violate these defined and accepted competencies. Third, established practices in the theory and practice of counseling that violate these competencies need to be modified or discontinued, which will be difficult for those trained in counseling during a time when multiculturalism was marginalized. Fourth, these competencies define a level playing field for counseling professionals from a variety of different cultural backgrounds, which will lead to still further changes in the theory and practice of counseling in which minority groups will have greater visibility. Fifth, these multicultural competencies will prepare the profession of counseling to fit with other cultures around the world who, because of urbanization and modernization, are increasingly looking to "counseling" as a means of managing social problems.

This book builds on a tradition going back to the 1982 document by Division 17 in a continuous effort by concerned counselors to better define those competencies that make counseling meaningful in a multicultural context. This is a continuing effort that will require modification to become more inclusive of the many different cultural contexts in which counseling is practiced. This book brings the reader "up to speed" by discussing competency and culture, defining the basic terms, identifying the problems of incompetency, describing the professional barriers to multiculturalism among counseling professionals, and defining the specific competencies from the viewpoint of different worldviews.

The *Multicultural Aspects of Counseling* series has emphasized the generic importance of culture-centered competencies in a variety of different populations and with regard to different problems addressed elsewhere in the series. This book provides a basic "map" or guidebook for identifying where the other extensive publications on multicultural counseling fit in the profession. The book will be an extremely important addition to every counselor's library.

Paul Pedersen, Ph.D.
Syracuse University
and Series Editor: Multicultural Aspects of Counseling

Preface

We have come a long way on our journey toward developing, measuring, and implementing multicultural counseling competencies in the mental health professions. Since the publication of the Division of Counseling Psychology (17) Education and Training Committee report, *Position Paper: Cross-Cultural Counseling Competencies* (Sue et al., 1982), the call for infusing multicultural competency criteria into standards of practice has been vocal, loud, and compelling. Yet, as a whole, the profession has not always been a willing participant in the recognition, endorsement, or infusion of multiculturalism into our standards of practice, code of ethics, and training programs. At best, the mental health professions can be characterized as unenlightened and reluctant to consider racial/cultural issues in counseling and psychotherapy; and, at worst, they have been downright hostile, antagonistic, and guilty of cultural oppression. The history of how counseling and psychotherapy have treated the culturally different in our society is a shameful one, filled with countless examples of pathologizing racial/cultural differences, victim blaming, stigmatizing and stereotyping minority populations, and using culturally biased methods of assessment and treatment, which have harmed and oppressed these populations. We recognize that these are strong allegations that arouse intense emotions in many of our colleagues. Yet, this book is about multicultural competence; and, multicultural competence demands that we take responsibility for and acknowledge potentially unpleasant aspects of our societal, professional, and individual histories.

This book is the work of a committee that was originally formed during a Division 17 open meeting of the Committee on Ethnic and Cultural Diversity. Many of us were disheartened at the slow progress made toward extending the original 1982 *Cross-Cultural Competencies* for adoption into counseling and clinical psychology programs. From that meeting, a subcommittee (Multicultural Counseling Competencies: Group II) was formed for the expressed purpose of (a) refining and extending the original competencies, (b) proposing the strategies and actions needed to implement the suggestions, and (c) disseminating our findings to the largest audience possible. Along with the support of Division 17, our task was also cosponsored by Division 45—The Society for the Psychological Study of Ethnic Minority Issues. Although originally formed in 1989, the work of the committee did not progress at a rapid pace because of major changes in the field since the early 1990s. Since the committee's formation, for example, important developments in multicultural counseling have occurred.

First, a number of major publications espousing standards of multicultural counseling competencies have come on the scene: *Multicultural Competencies/Standards: A Call to the Profession* (Sue, Arredondo, & McDavis, 1992); *Guidelines for Providers of Psychological Services to Ethnic, Linguistic, and Culturally Diverse Populations* (American Psychological Association, 1993); *Operationalization of the Multicultural Counseling Competencies* (Arredondo et al., 1996); *Multicultural Counseling Competencies: Assessment, Education and Training, and Supervision* (Pope-Davis & Coleman, 1997); *Handbook of Multicultural Counseling* (Ponterotto, Casas, Suzuki, & Alexander, 1995); *Toward a Culturally Competent System of Care* (Cross, Bazron, Dennis, & Isaacs, 1989); *Multicultural Organizational Development: Implications for the Counseling Profession* (Sue, 1995b); and *Developing Culturally Competent Systems of Care for State Mental Health Services* (Munoz & Sanchez, 1996).

Second, instruments have been developed to measure multicultural counseling competence at the individual level: The Cross-Cultural Counseling Inventory—Revised (LaFromboise, Coleman, & Hernandez, 1991), Multicultural Counseling Awareness Scale—Form B (Ponterotto, Sanchez, & Magids, 1991), Multicultural Counseling Inventory (Sodowsky, Taffe, Gutkin, & Wise (1992), and the Multicultural Awareness-Knowledge-Skills Survey (D'Andrea, Daniels, & Heck, 1991); and at the institutional level, Multicultural Competency Checklist (Ponterotto, Alexander, & Grieger, 1995) and the recent Multicultural Environment Inventory (Pope-Davis & Lui, 1995).

Third, as of this writing, six divisions of the American Counseling Association including the Association of Multicultural Counseling and Development and the Association for Counselor Education and Supervision and two divisions of the American Psychological Association (Division of Counseling Psychology-17 and Society for the Study of Ethnic Minority Issues-45) have officially endorsed the 1992 multicultural counseling competencies (Sue et al., 1992). Committees representing other divisions have also been formed to explore the possible implementation of multicultural competencies into certain standards of practice.

We have been most gratified at these positive changes but they necessitated altering our original publication plans. Rather than being redundant, we have chosen to produce a state-of-the-art book integrating the literature and work on multicultural counseling competencies and to draw out implications for individual, professional, and institutional development. We believe that *Multicultural Counseling Competencies: Individual, Professional, and Organizational Development* is the first attempt to trace the importance of integrating multicultural competencies in all three domains. As such, this text is appropriate for use in general introductory counseling/ therapy courses or ones on multicultural counseling and psychotherapy. Each chapter sequentially discusses what is required of mental health workers, service organizations, and educational training programs to be identified as "multiculturally competent."

Chapter 1 defines the term *multiculturalism* and provides a working definition from which counselors and therapists can ground their awareness, knowledge, and skills. Many terms related to multicultural counseling and therapy are also clarified. Chapter 2 describes a new concept called "ethnocentric monoculturalism" and how it has inundated our society and the mental health professions as well. This chapter provides a historical view of the Euro-American worldview. Chapter 3 forthrightly addresses counseling and counseling psychology's response to multiculturalism, identifies the major resistances encountered, and analyzes their sociopolitical meanings. Chapter 4 summarizes the 1992 multicultural counseling competencies (several new ones are proposed), but also breaks new ground by addressing the issue of multicultural organizational competence. Characteristics of the culturally inclusive and competent organization are presented. The next three chapters are sequentially organized to deal with specific cultural competencies related to the Euro-American worldview (Chapter 5), the racial/ethnic minority worldviews (Chapter 6), and culturally appropriate intervention strategies (Chapter 7). Chapter 7 is especially interesting because we discuss the need to play alternative roles in the helping process and the need to use the lessons from non-Western or indigenous healing systems and practices. We have devoted two chapters to multicultural organizational development (Chapters 8 and 9) for two reasons: (a) We believe strongly that it represents the next multicultural frontier, and (b) we believe that change at an individual level is not enough without changing the very institutions that so forcefully control our behaviors as individuals and professionals. Last, we end with Chapter 10, giving specific suggestions on how to develop multicultural competencies at the individual, professional, and institutional levels. We hope that students and professionals in the mental health fields will find this book of help in becoming more culturally competent.

Derald Wing Sue, Chair

1

What Is Multiculturalism and Multicultural Counseling and Therapy?

MULTICULTURAL COUNSELING COMPETENCE IS . . .

- Being able to provide a working definition of multiculturalism:

    It values cultural pluralism, values diversity, and is a national resource and treasure.

    It is about social justice, cultural democracy, and equity.

    It helps us acquire the attitudes, knowledge, and skills needed to function effectively in a pluralistic society.

    It includes diversity in race, class, gender, ethnicity, sexual orientation, and so on.

    It involves our willingness to explore both the positive and negative aspects of all groups.

    It is an essential component of analytical thinking and challenges us to study multiple cultures, and to develop multiple perspectives.

    It is about a commitment to change social conditions that deny equal access and opportunities (social justice).

    It means change at the individual, institutional, and societal levels.

    It means owning up to painful realities about oneself, our group, and our society.

    It is about achieving positive individual, community, and societal outcomes.

- Being able to clearly define one's meaning of terms related to multiculturalism such as culture, race, ethnicity, diversity, minority, majority, and so on.

- Being able to define multicultural counseling and therapy and to translate it into practice.
- Being able to define the meaning of multicultural organizational development and to translate it into practical implications.

In the counseling profession, multiculturalism has been called the "fourth force in counseling" (Pedersen, 1991a, 1991b), although it might more correctly be described as a "fourth dimension" because all helping originates from a cultural context. Although the multicultural movement is viewed positively by many, others find it a threatening and frightening development in our society. The terms *multiculturalism* and *diversity* are often correctly or mistakenly associated with such labels as affirmative action, quotas, civil rights, discrimination, reverse discrimination, racism, sexism, anti-White, political correctness, and many other emotion-arousing terms.

The confusion associated with these concepts and the strong passions that are produced by them can be both productive and counterproductive. The civil rights movement, which preceded the passage of the 1964 Civil Rights Act, was born from passionate feelings and beliefs (riots, sit-ins, marches, and so on). At times, however, the deep emotions that many people have about multiculturalism may interfere with their ability to communicate information, to influence others via sensitivity and logic, and to win over potential allies. Likewise, many well-intentioned individuals who harbor mistaken notions about multiculturalism may feel equally passionate and work against it. The "hot rhetoric" and confrontations that arise are disturbing to groups of people and organizational equilibrium because they demand change. As a result, many of our professional organizations, educational institutions, mental health services, and counselor training programs have done little or only made cosmetic changes to avoid controversy and emotionalism. This reluctance to speak out on social justice issues and to take positive action have kept our profession and many organizations from making any major progress toward multiculturalism.

During the past three decades, the mental health counseling professions have increasingly called attention to the need for practitioners to develop multicultural counseling competencies (Sue, Arredondo, & McDavis, 1992; Sue et al., 1982). Indeed, many cross-cultural researchers now argue that every counseling encounter is multicultural in some way, and that multiculturalism is a new paradigm, "the fourth force in counseling," relevant across all fields of counseling as a generic, rather than "exotic" perspective (Fukuyama, 1990; Pedersen, 1991). The writings of many multicultural specialists seem to advocate that multiculturalism must include differences based on religion, sexual orientation, socioeconomic factors, age, gender, physical (dis)abilities, and even on levels of acculturation and assimilation (Atkinson, Morten, & Sue, 1993; Margolis & Runtga, 1986; Sue, Ivey, & Pedersen, 1996). This model introduces concepts of cultural filters and cultural relativity into the field of mental health, expanding traditional notions of illness and health considerably (Smith & Vasquez, 1985).

Some researchers, however, warn that concepts of multiculturalism can become diluted to the point of uselessness if the definition is expanded to include more than race and ethnicity (Locke, 1990; Smith & Vasquez, 1985). This warning is well taken, especially when used by individuals or society to divert attention away from matters related to racism, sexism, and homophobia. There is no doubt, as Helms (1994a, 1994b) warns, that broad definitions of multiculturalism obscure and ignore race, that this may be done intentionally and unintentionally, that it may allow White people to avoid dealing with their own biases, and that it continues to perpetuate misinformation in the professional literature. Nevertheless, our working definition of multiculturalism conceptually includes these various dimensions.

Those who support the multicultural paradigm suggest that it is complementary to the psychodynamic, behavioral, and humanistic frameworks of psychology and human development, all of which have developed from European/American traditions and research (Highlen, 1996; Sue et al., 1996). These research traditions have focused primarily on the intrapsychic factors affecting human development, and have left the study of cultural influences on people to anthropologists and sociologists (Smith & Vasquez, 1985). Now, however, counseling and counseling psychology have begun to make use of the insights from other fields. Despite these insights, considerable confusion continues to surround the meaning of multiculturalism and multicultural competence.

A Postmodern Definition of Multiculturalism

As will be discussed in Chapter 2, most of Western science is based on what has been called "modernism," an epistemology characterized by rational, linear, positivist, and empirical traditions in Western science (Gergen, 1994; Gonzalez, 1997; Highlen, 1996; Hoshmand, 1989). Simply put, it is believed that one can study phenomena objectively, that the universe operates under linear cause-effect laws, that measurements will remain constant, and that universal statements of truths exist. Many multi-cultural psychologists have begun to believe that the focus on empirical reality is overly restrictive, narrow, and represents only one worldview. These epistemological assumptions, indeed, are not necessarily shared by non-Western cultures and societies in which social reality reflects one's worldview about the nature of human inquiry (Christopher, 1996; Sue et al., 1996).

The multicultural movement in psychology and education is truly "post-modern" in that it entertains the existence of multiple belief systems and multiple perspectives (Gonzalez, 1997). As such, it may encompass "social constructionism" in which meanings and the view of "reality" are developed through social interaction (the networks of social agreements) and "constructivism" or how personal realities are constructed. Consistent with the postmodern philosophy of science, several assumptions inherent in multiculturalism can be identified (Gonzalez, 1997; Highlen, 1996; Sue et al., 1996):

1. Multiculturalism accepts the existence of multiple worldviews. There are many alternative ways to ask and answer questions about the human condition besides the positivist/logical paradigm. Worldviews are neither "good or bad" nor "right or wrong."

2. Multiculturalism embodies social constructionism, meaning that people construct their worlds through social processes (historical, cultural, and social experiences) that contain cultural symbols and metaphors. Cultural relativism becomes an important concept because it implies that each culture is unique and must be understood in itself and not by reference to any other culture. Furthermore, it validates a sociopolitical stance in recognizing the unfairness of one group imposing its standards on another.

3. Multiculturalism is contextualist in that behavior can only be understood within the context of its occurrence. In psychology, it challenges a "universal psychology" because all theories of counseling and psychotherapy, for example, arise from a particular cultural context and may not be applicable to another.

4. Multiculturalism offers a "both/and" rather than an "either/or" view of the world. All worldviews or theories of counseling and psychotherapy are allowed to exist under an umbrella, even if they posit diametrically opposed principles. It is assumed that diverse worldviews or theories provide different perspectives of the same phenomenon. Each perspective captures a different and valid view.

5. Multiculturalism extols a relational view of language, rather than a representational one. Because language is most strongly correlated with culture and the "perception of reality," a relational view most clearly allows for realities and truths beyond the Western scientific tradition.

A Working Definition of Multiculturalism:
Ten Characteristics

It is clear that the postmodern definition of multiculturalism offers us the philosophical underpinnings of the movement. Although valuable in itself, translating this dynamic, organic, and evolving concept into practical implications may be difficult without a working definition. In keeping with postmodern philosophy, it is important to note that the precise definition of multiculturalism is continually evolving, and the language used to describe its characteristics and processes also continues to change. Before discussing the specifics of multicultural competence, it is important for us to translate multiculturalism into a working definition. We have identified 10 major characteristics of multiculturalism.

1. Multiculturalism values cultural pluralism and acknowledges our nation as a cultural mosaic rather than a melting pot. It represents a major revolution that promises to overcome ethnocentric notions in our society. It teaches the valuing of diversity rather than negation or even "toleration." Multiculturalism is not a "national burden" but a "national resource and treasure."

2. Multiculturalism is about social justice, cultural democracy, and equity. It is consistent with the democratic ideals of the Declaration of Independence, the U.S. Constitution, and the Bill of Rights. Although these documents have been intended for only an elite few at our nation's birth, multiculturalism seeks to actualize these ideals for all groups.

3. Multiculturalism is about helping all of us to acquire the attitudes, knowledge, and skills needed to function effectively in a pluralistic democratic society and to interact, negotiate, and communicate with peoples from diverse backgrounds.

4. Multiculturalism is reflected in more than just race, class, gender, and ethnicity. It also includes diversity in religion, national origin, sexual orientation, ability and disability, age, geographic origin, and so forth. Each of these characteristics contributes to our individual and collective diversity.

5. Multiculturalism is about celebrating the realistic contributions and achievements of our and other cultures. It also involves our willingness to explore both the positive and negative aspects of our group's and other groups' behavior over time. It appreciates the complexity of lived experience. It means becoming actively involved in seeking to understand the history, conditions, and social reality of the multiple groups in our society.

6. Multiculturalism is an essential component of analytical thinking. It is not about advocating an orthodoxy or dogma, but rather about challenging us to study multiple cultures, to develop multiple perspectives, and to teach our children how to integrate broad and conflicting bodies of information to arrive at sound judgments.

7. Multiculturalism respects and values other perspectives, but it is not value neutral. It involves an activist orientation and a commitment to change social conditions that deny equal access and opportunities (social justice). As such, it recognizes that "treating everyone the same" may deny equal access and opportunities, and that differential treatment is not necessarily "preferential." It involves investigating differences in power, privilege, and the distribution of scarce resources as well as rights and responsibilities.

8. Multiculturalism means "change" at the individual, organizational, and societal levels. It encourages us to begin the process of developing new theories, practices, policies, and organizational structures that are more responsive to all groups. As such, it is an ongoing and long-term process that requires commitment and hard work.

9. Multiculturalism may mean owning up to painful realities about oneself, our group, and our society. It may involve tension, discomfort, and must include a willingness to honestly confront and work through potentially unpleasant conflicts.

10. Multiculturalism is about achieving positive individual, community, and societal outcomes because it values inclusion, cooperation, and movement toward mutually shared goals.

Although changing to a multicultural entity may be occasionally unpleasant, the potential benefits are many. People who become increasingly multicultural in outlook often remark that they have personally benefited. They have experienced a broadening of their horizons, an increased appreciation of people (all colors and cultures), become less afraid and intimidated by differences, and have been able to communicate more openly and clearly with their family, friends, and coworkers. Thus, their effectiveness in relating to others has improved their lives and their functioning in a pluralistic society as well. Likewise, a society that values multiculturalism is one that makes use of all its resources and maximizes the contributions of all groups. A harmonious and inclusive society allows our children to acquire the knowledge and skills necessary for them to function and contribute as productive citizens in a pluralistic society and global world.

In summary, multiculturalism is both a philosophical and practical orientation to the study, understanding, and valuing of multiple worldviews related to major biological, cultural, ethnic, and other sociodemographic groupings. Although the philosophical basis of multiculturalism is related to postmodernism, the practical orientation speaks to the practice of individual, institutional, and societal changes that provide for equal access and opportunities for all groups in our society. In this definition, multiculturalism is conceptually meant to include the broad range of significant differences that so often hinder communication and understanding among people, but will most often be discussed in terms of ethnic and racial differences, as representing some of the most problematic divisions in U.S. culture. A true multicultural perspective balances the extremes of universalism and relativism by explaining behavior as a function of those culturally learned perspectives that are unique to a particular group and to those common-ground universals that are shared across groups. The goal of this book is to describe a synergy of universal and relativistic perspectives.

Definitions and Terms Related to Multiculturalism

There are many terms that are used synonymously or in conjunction with multiculturalism. Misuse, or lack of consensus in usage, can be problematic and can lead to miscommunication and misunderstanding. We will attempt to define terms such as culture, race, ethnicity, diversity, and so on; however, it is important to note that our definitions may differ from others.

Culture

There are many definitions of *culture,* which generally refer to "an integrated pattern of human behavior that includes thoughts, communications, actions, customs, beliefs, values, and institutions of a racial, ethnic, religious, or social group" (Cross, Bazron, Dennis, & Isaacs, 1989, p. iv). These patterns may be explicit or implicit and are transmitted via socialization processes. Linton's (1945) definition of culture is perhaps the most succinct: "the configuration of learned behavior and results of behavior whose components and elements are shared and transmitted by the members of a particularly society." There are several important points to be made about our definition of culture.

First, culture is not synonymous with "race" or "ethnic group." Jewish, Polish, Irish, and Italian Americans represent diverse ethnic groups who may share a common racial classification. Yet, their cultural matrices may be far different from one another. Likewise, an Irish and Italian American, despite possessing different ethnic heritages, may share the same cultural matrix. And, small groups of individuals within the same ethnic group may develop behavior patterns they share and transmit, which in essence constitute a form of culture.

Second, every society or group that shares and transmits behaviors to its members possesses a culture. Euro-Americans, African Americans, Latino/ Hispanic Americans, Asian Americans/Pacific Islanders, Native Americans, and other social groups have a culture. Thus, the use of terms such as "culturally deprived," "culturally impoverished," "culturally deficient," and "culturally disadvantaged" to describe racial/ethnic minority groups are inaccurate, demeaning, and ethnocentric. These conceptual terms imply that certain groups have no culture when in actuality they ethnocentrically imply that certain minority groups "do not have the right culture!"

Race

Much confusion surrounds the definition and usage of *race*. The term first appeared in the English language less than 300 years ago and has become much misused, misunderstood, and maligned since then (Atkinson et al., 1993). The two dominant definitions of race are based on either a constellation of biological and physical traits or internal/external social perspectives.

Biological definitions. Biologists and some social scientists tend to prefer a definition that recognizes three basic racial types predicated on a biological/ hereditary classification: Caucasoid, Mongoloid, and Negroid. Krogman (1945) defines race as "a subgroup of peoples possessing a definite combination of physical characteristics of genetic origin, the combination of which to varying degrees distinguishes the subgroup from other subgroups of mankind" (p. 49). These physical characteristics include but are not limited to skin pigmentation, head form, facial features, and color and texture of body hair.

There are many problems associated with attempting to classify people along these three schemes. First, there appears to be many more similarities between groups than differences (we all originated from a single genus species—homo sapiens), and many more differences within racial groups than between them. Second, biological definitions assume inbreeding among geographically isolated groups, which lead to and perpetuate distinguishable physical traits among the three races. Yet, common gene pools have not been in existence for some time due to frequent migrations, invasions, and explorations by various racial groups (Schaefer, 1988; Zuckerman, 1990). For example, most African Americans have so-called "White blood" in them. Latinos/Hispanics, depending on point of geographical origin, can be representative of any of the three races. The vast majority of Latinos in the United States are indigenous (Indian), mestizo (Indian and Spanish), or mulatto (African and Spanish). Most of the population of Mexican origin in the United States are indigenous/mestizo and, although they may not acknowledge it, also have African blood stemming from the colonial period. Increasingly, social scientists are having to cope with the reality of biracial/multiracial individuals who defy traditional classification systems (Root, 1992, 1996). Third, biologists are in disagreement among themselves as to how many races exist in the world, with estimates ranging from 3 to 200 (Schaefer, 1988). In essence, little agreement about the criteria defining race in a biological manner exists.

Social definitions. Atkinson et al. (1993) make a specific point that race as a biological concept is used for classification and has no biological consequence; however, what people believe about race has major social consequences. External societal definitions of race have often resulted in ideological racism, which links physical characteristics of groups (usually skin color) to major psychological traits (Feagin, 1989). For example, the expressed beliefs of Al Campanis (former Dodger executive) and former sportscaster Jimmy "The Greek" Snyder that Blacks are "great athletes" but "poor scholars" are sentiments that have shaped U.S. treatment of African Americans. Likewise, attributing lower intelligence and inferior psychological characteristics to one "racial group" and attributing positive traits to another have profound social consequences related to power and privilege. Societal definitions are often determined by ethnocentric and privilege considerations. The "one-drop rule" dictated that if you even had one drop of Black blood (offspring of mixed marriages/relatives with Black ancestors) you were considered "Black." Ironically, the federal government requires that to be American Indian, the person must have 25% blood quantum of Indian "blood." This latter ploy may be seen as an attempt by the U.S. government to escape certain economic obligations to American Indians.

Although these examples of social definitions may be seen as examples of how society maintains political oppression of racial groups, race remains an important psychological and political concept (Helms & Richardson, 1997). This is especially true with respect to "racial self-identification" in which groups define themselves racially by certain physical features highly correlated in social relations with others. "Regardless of its biological validity, the concept of race has taken on important social meaning in terms of how outsiders view members of a 'racial' group and how individuals within the 'racial' group view themselves, members of their group, and members of other 'racial' groups" (Atkinson et al., 1993, p. 7). Although the sociopolitical complexity of defining race must be acknowledged, we will refer to five major groupings in the socioracial manner proposed by Carter (1995), Helms (1994a), and Helms and Richardson

(1996): African Americans, Asian Americans/Pacific Islanders, Latino/ Hispanic Americans, Native Americans, and White Americans.

Ethnicity

Ethnicity has both a broad and narrower definition. The broad definition includes both cultural and physical features and, as a result, is often used interchangeably with race. We prefer to use the term in the narrower sense of "common ancestral origin" on the basis of at least one of their national or cultural characteristics. Thus, an ethnic group is one in which the members share and transmit a unique cultural and social heritage passed on from one generation to the next; these cultural patterns (differences in nationality, customs, language, religion) are more related to national origin rather than physical differences, which may or may not be germane. Ethnicity does not have a biological or genetic foundation and should not be used synonymously with race. Ponterotto and Casas (1991) state, "Jews, given their shared social, cultural, and religious heritage are an ethnic group; they are not, however, a race."

Diversity

Diversity is not multiculturalism, although it may be a necessary but not a sufficient condition to achieve the latter. For example, one can have a diverse workforce, diverse school system, or a diverse clientele and still be monocultural. This is especially true when women may make up 50% of an organization, but few are represented in upper management. *Diversity* is a term that originally was used to describe the changing worker characteristics of the future (Packer & Johnston, 1987). Such differences as race, ethnicity, gender, sexual orientation, age, religion, and physical ability or disability became associated with these defining characteristics. Diversity speaks to the presence or absence of numerical symmetry of these differences in our society. It is broad in description and may be overused causing a great deal of confusion. Some have advocated a separation between multicultural distinctions (reserved only for race, ethnicity, and culture) and the term diversity (reserved for all other people differences) (Arredondo et al., 1996).

Our previous definition of multiculturalism and our belief that differences associated with sexual orientation and the fact that some physically challenged individuals (deafness) can legitimately claim to be culturally distinct make such a distinction difficult. Rather, we prefer to use the term diversity in either the broad sense when that is our intent, or to specify the type of diversity we are speaking about (i.e., race, sexual orientation, gender, age).

Minority

In this book we will use the definition of *minority* posed by Wirth (1945):

> a group of people who, because of physical or cultural characteristics, are singled out from the others in society in which they live for differential and unequal treatment, and who therefore regard themselves as objects of collective discrimination. (p. 347)

This definition makes no reference to numerical size; in other words, it is possible to be a minority group even when your numbers are greater than any other group (à la South Africa, where 80% of inhabitants are Black, but they are still considered a minority group). The defining features of minority status are oppression by society by virtue of group membership; restriction in educational, economic, and political opportunities; and the lack of externally sanctioned power to address the inequities. According to Atkinson et al. (1993) this definition is preferred because it includes women as well. Thus, when reference is made to "racial/ethnic minorities," we are referring to groups of people who are singled out for collective discrimination based on physical characteristics or ancestry.

It is important to note that some prefer the use of "visible racial, ethnic group" (VREG) as a means to indicate the importance of visible physical differences (Cook & Helms, 1988). Although it poses additional problems (self-identified racial minority but not visible members of the group), the authors make a strong case that skin color and other physical features dictate qualitatively different experiences. This is especially true when we define *majority group* in which White ethnics are also considered under this term.

Last, in our usage of the term minority we disavow any implications that it is equated with "less than," "inferiority," or "personal powerlessness." We understand the objections some of our colleagues express regarding the use of the term. Yet, our tentative use of the term is based on an internal definition by the minority group that defines the majority constituents in reference to unfair, unequal treatment fostered by society. In that manner, the negativism and locus of responsibility are placed on the "majority" group.

Majority

To speak of a minority group means that we must entertain the existence of a *majority* group as well (Ponterotto & Pedersen, 1993). In broad terms, the majority can be defined as the group that (a) holds the balance of economic, social, and political power; (b) controls the gateways to power and privilege; and (c) determines which groups will be allowed access to the benefits, privileges, and opportunities of the society. In the United States that term is generally reserved for White Euro-Americans as most represented by mainstream and/or dominant White Anglo-Saxons. Although considerable controversy surrounds the definition, the rationale for such a characterization has been attempted by many social scientists:

> If there is anything in American life that can be described as an overall American culture that serves as a reference point for immigrants and their children, it can be described . . . as the middle-class cultural patterns of largely White Protestant Anglo-Saxon origins. (Gordon, 1964)

> Majority group incorporates not only White, Anglo-Saxon Protestants, but also White ethnic groups . . . although most White immigrant groups were confronted with prejudice and oppression when first arriving in America, their experiences in the U.S. has been qualitatively different than the experiences of non-White people. (Ponterotto & Casas, 1991)

> In a significant way, European immigrants over the past century and Blacks face opposite cultural problems. The new Europeans were seen as not "American" enough; the dominant pressure on them was to give up their strange and threatening ways and to assimilate. Blacks were Americans of lower caste; the pressure on them was to "stay in their place" and not attempt assimilation into mainstream culture of the privileged. (Pettigrew, 1988, p. 24)

> White culture is the synthesis of ideas, values, and beliefs coalesced from descendants of White European ethnic groups in the United States. (Katz, 1985)

Multicultural Counseling and Therapy

If we accept the postmodern and working definitions of multiculturalism, and if we use the previous terms as intended via the clarifications, then, to be logically consistent, multicultural counseling/therapy can be defined in the following manner.

Multicultural counseling and therapy (MCT) is a metatheoretical approach that (a) recognizes that all modes and theories of helping arise from a particular cultural context; (b) refers specifically to a helping relation-ship in which two or more of the participants are of different cultural backgrounds; (c) includes any counseling combination that fulfills the definition of "culture"; (d) recognizes the use of both Western and non-Western approaches to helping; and (e) is characterized by the helping professional's culturally appropriate awareness, knowledge, and skills (Sue, 1995a; Sue et al., 1996).

Originally called "cross-cultural counseling/therapy," this usage has become progressively less popular and has been superseded by the term MCT. Because it is inclusive, MCT may mean different things to different people (racial/ethnic minorities emphasis, sexual orientation emphasis, gender emphasis, and so on); thus, it is very important for us to specify the particular populations we are referencing.

Multicultural Organizational Development

Multicultural organizational development (MOD) is a relatively new term, originally used in a business setting to facilitate using the full potential of a diverse workforce. All organizations whether business or industry, government, mental health agency, or educational institution have an organizational culture. Schein (1990) defines *organizational culture* as a pattern of basic assumptions that are invented, discovered, or developed by a particular group as it learns to cope with its problems of "external adaptation and internal integration" (p. 111). These patterns can then be taught to new members as the appropriate ways to perceive, think, and feel in relation to its problems. Thus, counselor education programs and community mental health agencies must be discussed not only in terms of their responses to a multicultural society, but also in relation to their own histories and internal cultures. Because these cultural values are firmly grounded in White male norms, they are monocultural in scope.

MOD attempts to change, refine, instill, or create new policies, pro-grams, practices, and structures that are multicultural; thus, moving the organization from a monocultural to a multicultural entity becomes the objective. To accomplish this goal, MOD "(a) takes a social justice per-spective (ending of oppression and discrimination in organizations); (b) believes that inequities that arise within organizations may be primar-ily due not to poor communication, lack of knowledge, poor management, person-organization fit problems, and so forth, but to monopolies of power; and (c) assumes that conflict is inevitable and not necessarily unhealthy" (Sue, 1995b, p. 482).

2

Ethnocentric Monoculturalism

MULTICULTURAL COUNSELING
COMPETENCE IS . . .

- Being able to define the five components of ethnocentric monoculturalism.

    Strong belief in the superiority of one group's cultural heritage over another

    Belief in the inferiority of all other groups' cultural heritage

    Possession of power to impose standards on the less powerful group

    Ethnocentric notions are manifested in the programs, policies, and structures of our institutions

    Operates as an invisible veil via cultural conditioning

- Possessing the knowledge and understanding of how the Euro-American worldview is reflected in the components of White culture.

- Being able to describe how the Western Euro-American worldview is reflected in traditional forms of counseling and psychotherapy.

- Being aware of the history and historical forces that shaped the multicultural/counseling movement.

Just as clarifying terms and concepts is important in Chapter 1, defining, recognizing, understanding, and becoming knowledgeable about the operation of "ethnocentric monoculturalism" becomes a necessity for the development of multicultural competence. This concept is much broader than racism, sexism, or homophobia, although it describes a process in which all three share common characteristics.

For example, it is becoming increasingly clear that the values, assumptions, beliefs, and practices of our society are structured in such a manner that they serve only one narrow segment of the population (Sue, Ivey, & Pedersen, 1996). Most teachers, counselors, and mental health professionals have not been trained to work with other than mainstream individuals or groups. This is understandable in light of the historical origins of education, counseling/guidance, and our mental health systems, which have their roots in Euro-American or Western cultures (Sue & Sue, 1990; Wehrly, 1995). As a result, American (U.S.) psychology has been severely criticized as being ethnocentric, monocultural, and inherently biased against racial/ethnic minorities, women, gays/lesbians, and other culturally different groups (Carter, 1995; Laird & Green, 1996; Ridley, 1995; Sue, Arredondo, & McDavis, 1992).

As voiced by many critics, our educational system and counseling/psychotherapy have often done great harm to our minority citizens. Rather than educate or heal, rather than to offer enlightenment and freedom, and rather than to allow for equal access and opportunities, historical and current practices have restricted, stereotyped, damaged, and oppressed the culturally different in our society. Yet, our nation and the mental health profession have continued to exhibit a strange resistance and inertia to addressing and ameliorating these problems.

In light of the increasing diversity of our society, mental health professionals will inevitably be encountering client populations that differ from them in race, culture, and ethnicity. Such changes, however, are believed to pose no problems as long as psychologists adhere to the notion of an unyielding universal psychology that is applicable across all populations. Although few mental health professionals would voice such a belief, in reality, the very policies and practices of mental health delivery systems do reflect such an ethnocentric orientation. The theories of counseling and psychotherapy, the standards used to judge normality-abnormality, and the actual process of mental health practice are culture bound and reflect a monocultural perspective of the helping professions (Highlen, 1994; Katz, 1985; Sue, 1990). As such, they are often culturally inappropriate and antagonistic to the lifestyles and values of minority groups in our society. Indeed, some mental health professionals assert that counseling and psychotherapy may be "handmaidens of the status quo," (Sue & Sue, 1990) "instruments of oppression," (Thomas & Sillen, 1972) and "transmitters of society's values" (Halleck, 1971).

We believe that "ethnocentric monoculturalism" is dysfunctional in a pluralistic society like the United States. Ethnocentric monoculturalism combines what Wrenn (1962, 1985) calls "cultural encapsulation" and Jones's (1972, 1997) description of "cultural racism." Five primary components can be identified.

1. First, there is a strong belief in the superiority of one group's cultural heritage (history, values, language, traditions, arts/crafts, and so on). The group norms and values are seen positively and descriptors may include such terms as "more advanced" and "more civilized." Members of the society may possess conscious and unconscious feelings of superiority and that their way of doing things is the "best way."

2. Second, there is a belief in the inferiority of all other groups' cultural heritage, which extends to their customs, values, traditions, and language. Other societies or groups may be perceived as "less developed," "uncivilized," "primitive," or even "pathological." The lifestyle or ways of doing things by the group are considered inferior.

3. Third, the dominant group possesses the power to impose their standards and beliefs on the less powerful group. This third component of ethnocentric monoculturalism is very important. All groups are to some extent ethnocentric; that is, they feel positively about their cultural heritage and way of life. Yet, if they do not possess the power to impose their values on others, they hypothetically cannot oppress. It is power or the unequal status relationship between groups that defines ethnocentric monoculturalism.

4. Fourth, the ethnocentric values and beliefs are manifested in the programs, policies, practices, structures, and institutions of the society. For example, chain-of-command systems, training and educational systems, communication systems, management systems, and performance appraisal systems often dictate and control our lives. They attain "untouchable and godfather-like" status in an organization. Because most systems are monocultural in nature and demand compliance, racial/ethnic minorities and women may be oppressed.

5. Fifth, because people are all products of cultural conditioning, their values and beliefs (worldview) represent an "invisible veil" that operates outside the level of conscious awareness. As a result, people assume universality—that the nature of reality and truth are shared by everyone regardless of race, culture, ethnicity, or gender. This assumption is erroneous, but seldom questioned because it is firmly ingrained in our worldview.

The last two characteristics of ethnocentric monoculturalism represent perhaps the greatest obstacles to a meaningful movement toward a multicultural society because they are often expressed unconsciously and unintentionally via our personal values/beliefs and our institutions.

Overcoming ethnocentric monoculturalism in our society, in general, and in the mental health field, in particular, is not an easy task. Becoming multiculturally competent requires commitment to the objectives enunciated by Sue et al. (1982), Sue et al. (1992), the American Psychological Association (1993), and Arredondo et al. (1996). Attaining these multicultural competencies must occur on a personal level, professional level, and an institutional level as well (Toporek & Reza, 1994). The objectives of multicultural competence are fourfold.

Objectives of Multicultural Competence

1. These objectives include having mental health professionals become culturally aware of their own values, biases, and assumptions about human behavior. What stereotypes, perceptions, and beliefs do they hold about culturally different groups that may hinder their ability to form a helpful and effective counseling/therapy relationship? What are the worldviews they bring to the clinical encounter? What value systems are inherent in the professional's theory of helping, and what values underlie the strategies and techniques used in the clinical situation? Without such an awareness and understanding, mental health professionals may inadvertently assume that everyone shares their worldview. When this happens, counselors and therapists may become guilty of cultural oppression, imposing values on their culturally different clients.

2. They include having mental health professionals acquire knowledge and understanding of the worldview of minority or culturally different groups and clients. What values, biases, and assumptions about human behavior do these groups hold? Is there such a thing as an African American, Asian American, Latino(a)/Hispanic American or American Indian worldview? Do other culturally different groups (women, the physically challenged, gays/lesbians, and so on) also have different worldviews. How might this affect assessment/therapeutic processes and goals? Knowledge of the history, life experiences, cultural values, and the hopes, fears, and aspirations of culturally different groups in the United States are crucial to becoming a culturally competent helper.

3. These objectives include having mental health professionals begin the process of developing appropriate and effective intervention strategies in working with culturally different clients. This means prevention as well as remediation approaches, and systems intervention as well as traditional one-to-one relationships. Equally important is the ability to make use of existing indigenous-helping/healing approaches, which may already exist in the minority community.

4. The objectives also include having mental health professionals understand how organizational and institutional forces may either enhance or negate the development of multicultural competence. In other words, it does little good that mental health practitioners are culturally competent when the very organizations that employ them are filled with monocultural

policies and practices. In many cases, organizational customs do not value or allow the use of cultural knowledge or skills. Some organizations may even actively discourage, negate, or punish multicultural expressions. Thus, it is imperative to view multicultural competence for organizations as well. Developing new rules, regulations, policies, practices, and structures that enhance multiculturalism within organizations are important.

This chapter explores the sociopolitical and historical forces behind ethnocentric monoculturalism in our society and mental health systems. It's primary goal is directed toward the first objective of becoming more culturally aware of how one's cultural conditioning and the sociopolitical forces of society affect worldview. It briefly traces the roots of the multicultural psychology movement, provides a rationale for the urgent need to adopt multicultural counseling/therapy standards, and outlines needed steps our profession must take if it is to become relevant and fulfill the promise of truly helping others.

The Euro-American Worldview

In general, worldviews are neither right-wrong nor good-bad. Even attempting to characterize some as more accurate is fraught with hazards. In our opinion, all worldviews represent legitimate perspectives that affect how we think, make decisions, define events, and behave (Christopher, 1996). In other words, they may be defined as how people perceive their relationship to the world (nature, other people, institutions, and so on). Worldviews are highly correlated with a person's cultural upbringing, sociopolitical history, and life experiences (Sue, 1977, 1978); they represent our philosophy of life and how we think the world operates (Ivey, Ivey, & Simek-Morgan, 1993). Thus, how society perceives race, culture, ethnicity, gender, sexual orientation, and so forth becomes an important determinant of a worldview as well (Carter, 1995).

Worldviews, in and of themselves, are monocultural by nature. If, however, we accept the premise that worldviews are neither right nor wrong, then a similar conclusion must be drawn about monoculturalism. Individuals with a Euro-American worldview in the United States will find their beliefs and values constantly validated because they are functioning within their own cultural context. Problems arise, however, when people's worldviews differ from the mainstream worldview and they are oppressed and victimized because of this difference. This is what we refer to as *ethnocentric monoculturalism*, which can be manifested in any society. Although there is nothing pathological about the Euro-American worldview, its ethnocentric monocultural manifestations have done much harm to culturally different groups in the United States. To understand this statement and to begin the process of becoming increasingly multicultural in our perspectives, it is important to obtain some understanding of the origins of the European-American worldview in psychology.

Origins

The European-American worldview is most reflected in what Katz (1985) refers to as the components of White culture (see Figure 2.1). Rugged individualism, competition, mastery and control over nature, a unitary and static conception of time, religion based on Christianity, separation of science and religion, and competition are a few of the values and beliefs indicative of this orientation. The development of this worldview has been said to be influenced by a host of sociopolitical occurrences (Highlen, 1994; Ramirez, 1983). First, the European colonization efforts toward the Americas operated from the assumption that the enculturation of indigenous peoples was justified because European culture was superior. Forcing the colonized to adopt European beliefs and customs was seen as "civilizing" them. Such a belief is also reflected in Euro-American culture and has been manifested in attitudes toward racial/ethnic minority groups in the United States. "Racial/ethnic minorities would not encounter problems if they assimilate and acculturate." Second, both the democratic and industrial revolutions led to the valuing of egalitarianism, individualism, and secularism. Where once the primary unit of identity was derived from the group, with traditions and rituals being an important aspect of expressing that unity, "individualism" operated to separate people from others and the universe. Third, spurred by major scientific discoveries such as those of Galileo (earth was not the center of the universe), and Darwin (survival of the fittest), a separation of science and religion began to occur. Although the Euro-American perspectives continued to evolve toward a much more rational, linear, analytic, and reductionistic character most exemplified by Western science's worship of the "experimental design," most non-Western European cultures continued to conceptualize the world from a holistic, collectivistic, and spiritual perspective.

Monocultural ethnocentric bias also has a long history in the United States and is even reflected as early as the uneven application of the *Bill of Rights* in favor of White immigrants/descendants as opposed to "minority" populations. Some 221 years ago, Britain's King George III accepted a *Declaration of Independence* from former subjects residing in this country. This proclamation was destined to shape and reshape the geopolitical and sociocultural landscape of the world over many times. The lofty language penned by its principal architect, Thomas Jefferson, and

Rugged Individualism
Individual is primary unit
Individual has primary responsibility
Independence and autonomy highly valued
    and rewarded
Individual can control environment

Competition
Winning is everything
Win/lose dichotomy

Action Orientation
Must master and control nature
Must always do something about a
    situation
Pragmatic/utilitarian view of life

Communication
Standard English
Written tradition
Direct eye contact
Limited physical contact
Control emotions

Time
Adherence to rigid time
Time is viewed as a commodity

Holidays
Based on Christian religion
Based on White history and male leaders

History
Based on European immigrants'
    experience in the United States
Romanticize war

Protestant Work Ethic
Working hard brings success

Progress and Future Orientation
Plan for future
Delayed gratification
Value continual improvement and progress

Emphasis on Scientific Method
Objective, rational, linear thinking
Cause and effect relationships
Quantitative emphasis

Status and Power
Measured by economic possessions
Credentials, titles, and positions
Believe "own" system
Believe better than other systems
Owning goods, space, property

Family Structure
Nuclear family is the ideal social unit
Male is breadwinner and the head of the
    household
Female is homemaker and subordinate to
    the husband
Patriarchal structure

Aesthetics
Music and art based on European cultures
Women's beauty based on blonde,
    blue-eyed, thin, young
Men's attractivenesss based on athletic
    ability, power, economic status

Religion
Belief in Christianity
No tolerance for deviation from single god
    concept

Figure 2.1. The Components of White Culture: Values and Beliefs

SOURCE: Katz, 1985. Copyright © 1985 by Sage Publications, Inc.

signed by those present was indeed inspiring: "We hold these truths to be self evident, that all men are created equal."

Yet, as we now view the historic actions of that time, we cannot but be struck by the paradox inherent in those events. First, all 56 of the signatories were White males of European descent, hardly a representation of the current racial and gender composition of the population. Second, the language of the declaration suggests that only men were created equal, but what about women? Third, many of the founding fathers were slave owners who seemed not to recognize the hypocritical personal standards they used because they considered Blacks to be subhuman. Fourth, the history of this land did not start with the *Declaration of Independence* or the formation of the United States of America. Yet, our textbooks continue to teach us an ethnocentric perspective, "Western civilization," which ignores over two thirds of the world's population. Last, it is important to note that those early Europeans who came to this country were immigrants attempting to escape persecution (oppression), but in the process did not recognize their own role in the oppression of indigenous peoples (American Indians) who had already resided in this country for centuries.

We do not take issue with the "good intentions" of the early founders. Nor do we infer in them evil and conscious motivations to oppress and dominate others. Yet, the history of the United States has been the history of oppression and discrimination against racial/ethnic minorities and women. Western European cultures, which formed the fabric of the United States of America, are relatively homogeneous when compared not only to the rest of the world, but to the increasing diversity in this country. This Euro-American worldview continues to form the foundations of our educational, social, economic, cultural, and political systems.

As more and more White immigrants came to the North American continent, the guiding principle of blending the many cultures became codified into such terms as "the melting pot" and "assimilation/acculturation" (Sue & Sue, 1990). The most desirable outcome of this process was a uniform and homogeneous consolidation of cultures—in essence, to become monocultural. Many psychologists of color, however, have referred to this process as "cultural genocide," an outcome of colonial thought (Guthrie, 1976; Sue & Sue, 1990; Thomas & Sillen, 1972; White & Parham, 1990). Wehrly (1995) states that "cultural assimilation, as practiced in the United States, is the expectation by the people in power that all immigrants and people outside the dominant group will give up their ethnic and cultural values and will adopt the values and norms of the dominant society—the White, male Euro-Americans" (p. 24).

The Western Euro-American Worldview
in Counseling/Therapy

Just as the Euro-American worldview is reflected throughout our society, Western psychology is characterized by an assumption that it is universal (pancultural, panethnic, and gender free) and that the human condition is governed by universal principles. Underlying Euro-American psychology are the assumptions of cultural superiority, secularism, and the values of individualism and egalitarianism. As a result, the cultural components of Western counseling and psychotherapy encompass the following characteristics: (a) healthy functioning is equated with autonomy and independence, (b) clients can and should master and control their own lives and the universe, and (c) self-awareness and personal growth are goals of the therapeutic process. These culture-bound values of counseling and psychotherapy have been described in greater detail elsewhere (Highlen, 1994, 1996; Katz, 1985; Sue et al., 1996; Sue & Sue, 1990) and are outlined in Figure 2.2.

Again, it is not whether these attributes of Western helping are good or bad but, rather, a matter of their appropriateness when applied to culturally different groups. Suffice it to say that many racial/ethnic groups consider healthy functioning to be equated with interdependence and collectivism, "being" in harmony with the universe rather than mastering it, and a concern with group rather than self-development and growth. When the Euro-American worldview in psychology is used to determine normality and abnormality, then the cultural values of racial/ethnic minority groups may appear "pathological." When practiced therapeutically with minority populations, counseling and psychotherapy may be truly described as a form of cultural oppression (Sue & Sue, 1990).

The Multicultural Counseling/Therapy (MCT) Movement

Although the term *multicultural counseling/therapy* (MCT) is of recent vintage, the phenomena of multiculturalism and cross-cultural communications may be as old as human history itself (Thompson, 1989). Jackson (1995) states the following:

Multiculturalism has an established history. For centuries, people of different cultural backgrounds have recognized the existence of problems associated with communicating with people from other cultural backgrounds. American society is not unique in its concern over multicultural issues. The real issue

Culture	Middle Class	Language
Standard English	Standard English	Standard English
Verbal communication	Verbal communication	Verbal communication
Individual centered	Adherence to time schedules (50-minute sessions)	
Verbal/emotional/behavioral expressiveness	Long-range goals	
Client-counselor communication	Ambiguity	
Openness and intimacy		
Cause-effect orientation		
Clear distinction between physical and mental well-being		
Nuclear family		

Figure 2.2. Generic Characteristics of Counseling

SOURCE: Taken from *Counseling the Culturally Different: Theory and Practice* by D. W. Sue and D. Sue, copyright 1990. Reprinted by permission of John Wiley & Sons, Inc.

is to what extent a society is willing to venture to ensure that the traditions, customs, values, and beliefs of a people different from the dominant majority will be recognized. The guidance and counseling movement must not ignore the rich multicultural past. (p. 4)

The beginnings of MCT in the United States cannot be viewed apart from the historical forces that led to its creation. Our brief journey back into history and our attempt to learn from the lessons of the past, reveals the continuing conflicts of monoculturalism versus multiculturalism. Although there had always been minority mental health professionals who expressed disagreements with the assumptions and practices of Western psychology, it was not until the 1950s and 1960s that issues of culture and race became salient in the practice of therapy. The civil rights movement (passage of the Civil Rights Act of 1964) served as a major impetus for disenfranchised minority groups to demand relevant services. Attacks against psychotherapy as being primarily a "White middle-class activity," which oppresses persons of color, were replete in the literature (Katz, 1985; Grier & Cobbs, 1968; Thomas & Sillen, 1972). Many enlightened educators and psychologists began to suggest the need to make mental health services relevant to the culturally different (Vontress, 1971; Wrenn, 1962).

Just as the civil rights movement was a rebellion of the oppressed in our society, MCT is being fueled by a demographic revolution literally changing the complexion of our society. As such, the impetus for change will become increasingly consumer generated. As the demographics in our society have changed, greater and greater demand for multiculturalism and diversity have become the rallying cry for many disenfranchised groups.

Demographic Changes Affecting Multiculturalism

According to 1990 U.S. Census information, the population of the United States is undergoing radical demographic changes, which will continue well into the 21st century. By the year 2000, more than one third of the population is projected to be racial or ethnic minorities and they will make up approximately 45% of the public school population (Sue et al., 1992). In California, minority students already constitute more than 50% of the school-age population. Perhaps more significant, more than 75% of those people currently entering the U.S. workforce are women and racial/ethnic minorities.

A comparison of the U.S. Census data from 1980 to 1990 (see Table 2.1) reveals the differential rate of growth among the different racial/ethnic minority groups (U.S. Bureau of the Census, 1992). Over a period of 10 years, the non-White population has grown at a phenomenal rate (African American = 13.18%; Native Americans = 37.96%; Hispanic Americans = 53.02%; Asian American/Pacific Islanders = 107.71%) while the White population has slowed to 6.01%. The huge increase in visible racial/ethnic minority groups is due to the fact that the current immigration rates are the largest in U.S. history and to greater numbers of non-White births in the United States (Atkinson, Morten, & Sue, 1998). Although the U.S. Bureau of Census projects that racial/ethnic minorities will become a numerical majority by the year 2050, some private surveys believe this will happen by the year 2030 (Sue, 1996). Furthermore, within several short decades, Hispanic/Latino Americans will become the largest ethnic minority group in the United States, surpassing African Americans. As Sue et al. (1992) note, in the near future, "working with minority constituents will become the norm rather than the exception" for all counseling professionals (p. 478). It is clear that interethnic population shifts are changing as well and multiculturalism will less frequently be described just in terms of Whites versus minorities, but will more frequently include the complex interactions of minority groups that differ from one another by race, ethnicity, language, and level of assimilation/acculturation.

Table 2.1 United States Ethnic Census, 1980 and 1990

	Number[a]		Percentage Distribution		Change 1980-1990	
	1980	*1990*	*1980*	*1990*	*Number[a]*	*Percent-age*
All persons	226,546	248,709	100.00	100.00	22,163	9.78
Male	110,048	121,239	48.58	48.75	11,191	10.17
Female	116,498	127,470	51.42	51.25	10,972	9.42
Race						
White	188,372	199,686	83.15	80.29	11,314	6.01
Black	26,495	29,986	11.70	12.06	3,491	13.18
American Indian, Eskimo, Aleut	1,420	1,959	0.63	0.79	539	37.96
American Indian	1,364	1,878	0.60	0.76	514	37.68
Eskimo	42	57	0.02	0.02	15	35.71
Aleut	14	24	0.01	0.01	10	71.43
Asian or Pacific Islander	3,502	7,274	1.55	2.92	3,772	107.71
Chinese	806	1,645	0.36	0.66	839	104.09
Filipino	775	1,407	0.34	0.57	632	81.55
Japanese	701	848	0.31	0.34	147	20.97
Asian Indian	362	815	0.16	0.33	453	125.14
Korean	355	799	0.16	0.32	444	125.07
Vietnamese	262	615	0.12	0.25	353	134.73
Hawaiian	167	211	0.07	0.08	44	26.35
Samoan	42	63	0.02	0.03	21	50.00
Guamanian	32	49	0.01	0.02	17	53.13
Other Asian/Pacific Islander	n.a.	822	n.a.	0.33	n.a.	n.a.
Other race	6,758	9,805	2.98	3.94	3,047	45.09
Total	226,547	248,710	100.00	100.00	22,163	9.78
Hispanic origins[b]						
Hispanic origin	14,609	22,354	6.45	8.99	7,745	53.02
Mexican	8,740	13,496	3.86	5.43	4,756	54.42
Puerto Rican	2,014	2,728	0.89	1.10	714	35.45
Cuban	803	1,044	0.35	0.42	241	30.01
Other Hispanic	3,051	5,086	1.35	2.04	2,035	66.70
Not of Hispanic origin	211,937	226,356	93.55	91.01	14,419	6.80

SOURCE: U.S. Bureau of the Census (1992).
NOTE: Slight differences in some totals due to rounding.
a. In thousands.
b. Persons of Hispanic origin may be of any race.

3

The Profession's Response
to Multiculturalism

MULTICULTURAL COUNSELING
COMPETENCE IS . . .

- Being aware of how the history of our society and our profession frequently were culturally encapsulated.
- Being aware of how the mental health fields have traditionally perceived racial/ethnic differences, have engaged in cultural oppression, and have been slow to recognize the importance of multiculturalism in mental health practice.
- Being able to understand the sociopolitical meaning of resistance to multiculturalism and being able to present cogent and logical rebuttals to the objections raised.

The helping profession's response to diversity and multicultural issues has been a shameful one (Carter, 1995; Sue & Sue, 1990). Racist and ethnocentric notions were frequently manifested in the research, theory, and practice of psychology and education. G. Stanley Hall, first president of the American Psychological Association, described Africans, Indians, and Chinese as members of "adolescent races" and as being in an inferior stage of development. Such concepts as "genetic inferiority," "cultural deprivation," and "culturally impoverished" were used to explain how minority groups lacked either the "right" genes or the "right" culture to succeed in this society (Carter, 1995; Highlen, 1994; Sue & Sue, 1990; White & Parham, 1990). Cultural and racial differences became equated with deviancy and pathology.

Although progress has been made in recognizing race, culture, and ethnicity from a more realistic and positive perspective, the profession continues to resist the incorporation of multicultural formulations into mainstream psychology (Betancourt & Lopez, 1993; Ponterotto & Casas, 1991). Indeed, there is considerable evidence to suggest that many mental health professionals feel threatened by the challenge of diversity and appear to advocate a retreat from the progress of the past 50 years (Brown, 1996; Fowers & Richardson, 1996; Weinrach & Thomas, 1996). The difficulty of overcoming ethnocentric monoculturalism is aptly stated by Meyers, Echemendia, and Trimble (1991):

> As we stand at the threshold of the 21st century, mental health professionals, and psychologists more specifically, continue to be predominantly Caucasian; to be trained by predominantly Caucasian faculty members; and to be trained in programs in which ethnic issues are ignored, regarded as deficiencies, or included as an afterthought. (p. 5)

The education and training of psychologists and counselors continue to experience a major chasm between the recommendations of numerous conferences/committees/commissions and mental health education and practice. These recommendations have loudly declared that psychologists must be prepared to function in a multicultural, multiethinic, and multiracial society and that lack of such preparation in working with a culturally different population should be considered unethical (American Psychological Association, 1993; Korman, 1974; Presidents Commission on Mental Health, 1980). Yet, although many mental health professionals could agree on what was wrong with the profession, few training programs could operationally define the characteristics of the culturally sensitive and competent helping professional. The lack of a working definition made change in training institutions difficult.

Counseling and Counseling Psychology's Response

In 1980, the Division of Counseling Psychology's (Division 17) Education and Training Committee formed a Cross-Cultural Counseling Competencies Committee for the purpose of developing culturally relevant counseling competencies for possible adoption into graduate schools of counseling and clinical psychology. Then President, Allen E. Ivey, asked Derald Wing Sue to Chair the Education and Training Committee to study and make recommendations. The "Competencies" were approved by the Executive Committee and published in *The Counseling Psychologist* (Sue et al., 1982). In 1992, Thomas A. Parham, President of the Association for Multicultural Counseling and Development, again asked Derald Wing Sue to head the Professional Standards Committee for the expressed purpose of refining and further developing the 1982 competencies. The work of the group was considered of sufficient importance that it was jointly published in the *Journal for Multicultural Counseling and Development* and the *Journal for Counseling and Development* (Sue, Arredondo, & McDavis, 1992).

These publications have stimulated much debate among the counseling community because they (a) provided a strong rationale for a multicultural perspective in the helping professions, (b) developed specific multicultural standards and competencies that defined the culturally competent counselor, and (c) advocated a call for action in the implementation of standards for both the American Counseling Association (ACA) and the American Psychological Association (APA). Helms and Richardson (1997) believe these proposed "competencies have become a landmark in the field because they initially awakened theorists', researchers', and practitioners' attention to the reality that traditional Western approaches to counseling and psychotherapy minimized the unique contributions of clients' and therapists' sociodemographic and psychodemographic characteristics to the therapy process."

Ethnocentric Monoculturalism in Counseling: The Seven Deadly Resistances

Despite the call for a more culturally relevant approach to working with minority populations, the counseling profession has continued to resist the implementation or incorporation of these standards into their practice or accreditation guidelines. These resistances fall into several categorical barriers that seemed to unfold sequentially as the multicultural counseling movement matured. Beneath the surface of these arguments, however, lies the primary culprit—"ethnocentric monoculturalism."

Resistance 1—Current theories and the practice of counseling and psychotherapy are equally appropriate and applicable to all populations regardless of race, culture, ethnicity, gender, sexual orientation, and so forth. Good counseling is good counseling. Although some counselor educators (Brown, 1996) have taken issue with this statement, they apparently fail to realize that a theory of helping, whether it be behavioral, humanistic, cognitive, or so forth, views most people as being essentially the same. Each particular theory assumes that it is equally applicable across situations, problems, and populations.

Analysis—The universal perspective of mental health practice continues to be a strong force in the profession. The myth of sameness has been seriously challenged by work on worldviews (Ibrahim, 1985; Ivey, Ivey, & Simek-Morgan, 1993; Kluckhohn & Strodtbeck, 1961; Pedersen, 1988; Sue, 1978; Sue, Ivey, & Pedersen, 1996), minority identity development models (Atkinson, Morten, & Sue, 1993; Carter, 1990; Cross, 1971, 1991; Helms, 1984; Kim, 1981; Parham, 1989; Parham & Helms, 1981; Ruiz, 1990; Sue & Sue, 1990), White identity development models (Hardiman, 1982; Helms, 1984; Katz & Ivey, 1977; Ponterotto, 1988; Sabnani, Ponterotto, & Borodovsky, 1991), and culture-specific strategies in working with culturally different populations (Ivey, 1986; Paniagua, 1994; Ridley, 1984; Sue, 1990). The conclusions that can be drawn from these publications are that (a) not only do people and groups share commonalities by virtue of being homo sapiens, but they are also different from one another; (b) differences are dictated by individual uniqueness and reference group membership; and (c) no single or universal approach will be appropriate for all populations, problems, and situations. Race, culture, ethnicity, gender, and sexual orientation matter!

Resistance 2—Although there may be limitations to traditional forms of counseling and psychotherapy when applied to a culturally different population, we lack conceptually sound multicultural standards. Multiculturalists are good at telling us what is wrong but offer few concrete suggestions.

Analysis—Almost all the early work on multicultural counseling and therapy concentrated on assailing the biased deficit models applied to racial/ethnic minorities (Sue, Ito, & Bradshaw, 1984), underuse of mental health services by minority populations (Snowden & Cheung, 1990; Sue, McKinney, Allen, & Hall, 1975), conflict of values between the counseling process and those of ethnic minorities (Sue & Sue, 1977), and the failure of intrapsychic models to consider systemic factors (Gunnings & Simpkins, 1972). Assertions were made that the training programs needed to be changed and that therapists were culturally incompetent to work with a diverse population. Although many White mental health professionals acknowledged these limitations and weaknesses in training, their major excuse for not implementing change was the lack of standards to determine multicultural competence and effectiveness.

Even prior to the 1980s, however, there was work on the need for counselors to teach skills and assist minority clients in negotiating societal systems (Gunnings & Simpkins, 1972). Empowerment of clients was considered an intimate aspect of competent counseling (Helms & Richardson,

1997). With the publication of the cross-cultural competencies from Division 17 (Sue et al., 1982), it appeared that finally such excuses for lack of change would be overcome.

Resistance 3—The cross-cultural counseling competencies identified in the Sue et al. (1982) report are too general and nonspecific to be of much good. We have to wait until they are stated in greater detail.

Analysis—For nearly 15 years after the publication of the Division 17 cross-cultural competencies, they languished in the professional literature. Although well received and frequently discussed by the profession, neither the professional organizations nor individual training programs incorporated them into their standards of practice. Indeed, the 1982 standards became one of the most frequently cited publications in multicultural counseling literature (Ponterotto & Sabnani, 1989). It appears that the profession was willing to acknowledge their importance verbally, but consciously or unconsciously resisted their implications; if believed to be of major import, the standards of practice and ethical guidelines of both the ACA and the APA would have to change.

When pressed by multicultural specialists to infuse these competencies into accreditation requirements, many leaders of the profession suggested that they were too general and abstract. Greater clarity and specificity were needed. These very same leaders seemed not to make note of the fact that the current standards of practice for both the ACA and APA were also vague and general in nature. Should they, therefore, be held in abeyance until they became more precise as well?

To counteract these objections, the multicultural counseling competencies were refined and extended in a major publication expanding the original 11 competencies to 31 (Sue et al., 1992) and followed by another publication that operationalized them into measurable objectives (Arredondo et al., 1996). At the time of this writing, several divisions of the American Counseling Association (ACES, AADA, ASCA, AGLBIC ASGW, and IAMFC) and the American Psychological Association (Division of Counseling Psychology and Society for the Psychological Study of Ethnic Minority Issues) have endorsed the competencies. Although this is a positive sign in our profession, we continue to wonder why it took so long for the helping professions to accept the importance of such standards.

Resistance 4—The multicultural competencies are just too complex and detailed. It is unrealistic for any training program to incorporate these into the curriculum and it is just too unrealistic to believe any one individual could become culturally competent given the multitude of knowledge and skills required.

Analysis—Although there is some validity to these statements, proponents of MCT again saw it as the unconscious resistance to change. Instead of being too general, simplistic, and imprecise, objections now arose because they were too complex and detailed! Proponents countered with arguments that becoming multiculturally competent is not a simple matter but a complex one that requires continuing education and training. Cultural competence should be conceptualized as a developmental lifelong process and not a static one with an endpoint. Realistically, it will never be possible to completely acquire knowledge and understanding of all the different groups in the society. Becoming multiculturally competent, however, in even one culture different from your own increases overall cultural competence and sensitivity. Becoming multiculturally competent is also being able to realize one's limitations and is manifested in the counselor or therapist (a) seeking consultation, (b) seeking continuing education, or (c) referring out to someone competent in working with that specific population.

Resistance 5—It's all good and well that we have multicultural competencies, but for them to be useful, we need to be able to measure, evaluate, and research them.

Analysis—Excuses for not incorporating multicultural competence criteria in training programs and accreditation frequently were manifest in measurement and research objections. Prior to implementing change, instruments had to be developed that could measure these criteria to be conducive to research and evaluation. These objections were quickly put to rest when, in the early 1990s, a number of multicultural researchers developed instruments attempting to measure cross-cultural counseling competencies: The Cross-Cultural Counseling Inventory-Revised (LaFromboise, Coleman, & Hernandez, 1991), Multicultural Counseling Awareness Scale-Form B: Revised Self Assessment (Ponterotto, Sanchez, & Magids, 1991), Multicultural Counseling Inventory (Sodowsky, Taffe, Gutkin, & Wise, 1992), and the Multicultural Awareness-Knowledge-Skills Survey (D'Andrea, Daniels, & Heck, 1991). Thus, many measures of multicultural competence became available for research and evaluation purposes.

Resistance 6—We would like to incorporate these standards into our accrediting bodies and guidelines, but we should wait until other culturally different groups are included. Most of the multicultural standards speak to visible racial/ethnic minorities, but what about standards for women, gay/lesbians, the physically challenged, and so forth?

Analysis—This is a difficult objection to contend with because of the potential misunderstandings and conflicts it is likely to engender. Most multicultural counseling competencies have been developed with racial/

ethnic minorities as the major focus. Many groups such as gays/lesbians and the physically challenged have a legitimate basis for their claim that they possess a distinct culture, have experienced minority group status, and often require a different counseling approach that recognizes their multicultural life experiences. Although many of the racial/cultural identity models and the recommended multicultural standards appear to be applicable to them, they could be improved with a greater focus on sexual orientation, gender, and disability.

We acknowledge these legitimate issues and hope to reach out to further modify these competencies. Yet, there is a strange "divide and conquer" aspect to these objections when they come from the mainstream. To wait until other group-specific standards can be developed and incorporated into the multicultural competencies appears to be a stalling ploy aimed at pitting one group against another. On the surface, mainstream psychology can hold itself out as being "fairminded," "evenhanded," and concerned with "all oppressed groups" when, in reality, it prevents change in the current standards of practice. Such a view has been increasingly expressed by primarily White male psychologists (Fowers & Richardson, 1996; Weinrach & Thomas, 1996). If mainstream psychology really believed in this commitment, it would throw away all its current standards because they are monocultural in orientation and do not include "all oppressed groups." We call on all culturally different groups not to have the multicultural agenda sidetracked by these obvious sociopolitical ploys. Let's adopt these standards with the commitment that as other group competencies are developed, they too will find inclusion.

Resistance 7—Multiculturalism is not such a good thing after all. It represents reverse racism, quotas, and is anti-White. It is biased, unbalanced, and presents only one side of the picture. It does not acknowledge the many contributions of Euro-American culture and society. We are tired and offended by the hostility and aggressive manner communicated by multiculturalists.

Analysis—As the first six resistances are unmasked for what they are, mainstream psychology has increasingly been forced to directly attack the multicultural movement by characterizing it as unreasonable and by distorting its goals and values (Weinrach & Thomas, 1996). Others have even assailed it for portraying majority cultural norms as racist and oppressive by nature (Fowers & Richardson, 1996) and have attacked the proponents as being histrionic and insulting (Brown, 1996). They claim that European American ideals include a philosophical or moral opposition to racism and that "American society" should be given credit for its many positive virtues. The reason that multiculturalism has thrived in our society should be credited to the positive qualities of Euro-American culture. Let us briefly address these points.

First, multicultural antagonists (Weinrach & Thomas, 1996) fail to acknowledge that the multicultural perspective cannot be ascribed to any individual or school of thought. Yet, they consistently refer to, and criticize, the multicultural movement by characterizing it in the most extreme and negative manner. They claim it to be separatist, self-defensive, exclusionary, fails to recognize within-group differences, fosters stereotypes, and advocates that only minorities can counsel members of their own group. Weinrach and Thomas (1996) not only fail to understand multiculturalism, but do a grave disservice by presenting a misleading multicultural position that can only be weakly defended. They take the extreme end of multicultural and ethnic minority positions, characterizing the multicultural perspective with this extremity, and then pointing to problems or contradictions in their characterization. Likewise, use of such terms as "anti-White," and "reverse racism" are used to imply that multiculturalism is an extreme movement. The sociopolitical ploy is to maintain the status quo by derogating the movement, thereby negating the legitimacy of the issues raised.

Second, multicultural antagonists contend that "the multicultural movement unfairly characterizes Euro-American culture and history as being oppressive and racist and denies its contributions to human rights" (Fowers & Richardson, 1996). Accordingly, "multiculturalists should be indebted to a society that allows them an environment to flourish" (Fowers & Richardson, 1996). As we have seen from our historical journey, Euro-American principles of equality, respect, and tolerance were advocated but not necessarily practiced by our forefathers. A strong case can be made that "equality" as defined by Euro-Americans was detrimental to persons of color because it (a) considered racial minorities to be "less than human" and (b) allowed our forefathers to oppress while maintaining the illusion of being in favor of human equality. Barongan et al. (1997) state that

the natural and inalienable rights of individuals valued by European and European American societies generally appear to have been intended for European Americans only. How else can European colonization and exploitation of Third World countries be explained? How else can the forced removal of Native Americans from their lands, centuries of enslavement and segregation of African Americans, immigration restrictions on persons of color through history, incarceration of Japanese Americans during World War II, and current English-only language requirements in the United States be explained? These acts have not been perpetrated by a few racist individuals,

but by no less than the governments of the North Atlantic cultures to which
Fowers and Richardson contend that multiculturalism is indebted. If Euro-
American ideals include a philosophical or moral opposition to racism, this
has often not been reflected in policies and behaviors. (p. 654)

Exposing these realistic facts and events is not one-sided, unbalanced,
or unfair. Not owning up to our own personal biases and our history of
oppression is to deny sociopolitical reality and represents the true injustice. Multiculturalism has survived not because of Euro-American influences but in spite of it. Cultural competence calls for awareness of one's
own cultural biases and assumptions about human behavior. It also calls
for an awareness and understanding of one's cultural and historical heritage. Only through this awareness and consciousness will we become
liberated.

4

The Multicultural
Counseling Competencies

MULTICULTURAL COUNSELING
COMPETENCE IS . . .

- Awareness of own assumptions, values, and biases.
- Understanding the worldview of the culturally different client.
- Developing appropriate intervention strategies and techniques.
- Being able to define a multiculturally competent organization.
- Understanding how organizational and institutional forces may either enhance or negate the development of multicultural competence.
- Being able to define the major characteristics of the culturally competent and inclusive organization:
    Commitments are from the top levels
    Possesses operationalized written policy, mission or vision statement of multiculturalism
    Possesses a multicultural and diversity action plan
    Possesses an empowered superordinate or multicultural oversight team
    Actively solicits feedback from employee groups
    Builds accountability to multiculturalism into the system
    Infuses multicultural competence into evaluation criteria
    Provides mentoring and support networks for minority employees
    Encourages coalition building and networking among minorities and women
    Possesses a systematic and long-term commitment to educating the entire workforce
    Views the organization as a reflection of the wider community

Since the publication of the Division 17 Cross-Cultural Counseling Competencies (Sue et al., 1982) and their subsequent refinement by the Association of Multicultural Counseling and Development (Sue, Arredondo, & McDavis, 1992), many other calls for the infusion of cross-cultural/multicultural competencies into graduate schools of clinical/counseling psychology, counselor education, and social work have been replete in the literature. Not only have multiple measures been developed to assess multicultural counseling competencies (cf. the review by Ponterotto, Rieger, Barrett, & Sparks, 1994), but models for multicultural counselor training have also been increasingly developed and advocated (Carney & Kahn, 1984; Pedersen, 1994; Ridley, Mendoza, Kanitz, Angermeier, & Zenk, 1994; Sue, 1991).

Despite the contributions made over the past several decades, however, the research literature continues to reveal negative biases among counseling professionals and/or a continuing neglect of racial/cultural issues as they impact the helping process (Pinderhughes, 1989; Ridley, 1995; Solomon, 1992; Sue et al., 1992). As a result, most members of racial/ethnic minority groups remain underserved in therapy, they may continue to prematurely terminate their sessions, they may be unintentionally pathologized, and they may experience being oppressed rather than helped in the therapeutic process.

Although we tend to view prejudice, discrimination, racism, and sexism as overt and intentional acts of unfairness and violence, it is the unintentional and covert forms of bias that may be the greater enemy because it is unseen and more pervasive. Ridley (1995) addresses this point well, which, by the way, is equally applicable to ethnocentric monoculturalism:

> Unintentional behavior is perhaps the most insidious form of racism. Unintentional racists are unaware of the harmful consequences of their behavior. They may be well-intentioned, and on the surface, their behavior may appear to be responsible. Because individuals, groups, or institutions that engage in unintentional racism do not wish to do harm, it is difficult to get them to see themselves as racists. They are more likely to deny their racism. . . . The major challenge facing counselors is to overcome unintentional racism and provide more equitable service delivery. (p. 38)

Not only are individuals products of their cultural conditioning, but institutional values and practices often reflect the biases of the larger society. By implication, then, mental health/counselor training includes biased assumptions and beliefs that are transmitted to counselors in their professional training. Because the training often equates these biases with "standards of normality-abnormality" and what constitutes "therapeutic effectiveness," they operate as an invisible veil. They become unquestioned guidelines for clinical practice dictating to counselors what they should or should not do. For example, the goal of counselors is to help clients become "independent and autonomous" (maturity equated with individualism), counselors do not give advice and suggestions (it fosters dependency), counselors do not self-disclose (undue influence), and counselors do not accept gifts from clients (it obligates the therapist and objectivity may be lost). Although these rules may make rational therapeutic sense from a Euro-American perspective of counseling and psychotherapy, some culturally different groups find such guidelines to be part of helping effectiveness. Helms and Richardson (1997) state that

> multicultural counseling should refer to the integration of dimensions of client cultures into pertinent counseling theories, techniques, and practices with the specific intent of providing clients of all sociodemographic and psychodemographic variations with effective mental health services . . . multicultural competence in counseling and psychotherapy should refer to the capacity to read the various cultural dynamics of clients (and therapists) and to react to each of these aspects of cultures in a manner that best suits the client's mental health needs and the therapist's relevant skills. (p. 70)

To aid in this process, we have purposely reproduced the AMCD multicultural competencies in this chapter with some revisions and additions. This is especially true with respect to multicultural organizational competencies. These competencies are left as aspirational ideals and not operationalized. This has purposely been done because of several reasons: (a) it allows groups and individuals to operationalize them in a meaningful fashion to their needs and concerns; (b) it avoids being arbitrary and allows continuing research and debate to establish the specific parameters of multicultural competence; and (c) one such excellent attempt at operationalization has already been accomplished (Arredondo et al., 1996).

Becoming multiculturally competent means the ability to free one's personal and professional development from the unquestioned socialization of our society and profession. The three dimensions to work on involve attitudes and beliefs, knowledge, and skills (Carney & Kahn, 1984; Sue et al, 1992; Sue et al., 1982). The first dimension deals with counselors' attitudes and beliefs about race, culture, ethnicity, gender, and sexual orientation; the need to check biases and stereotypes; development of a positive orientation toward multiculturalism; and the way counselors' values and biases may hinder effective counseling and therapy. The second dimension recognizes that the culturally skilled helping professional is knowledgeable and understanding of his or her own worldview, has specific knowledge of the cultural groups he or she works with, and understands sociopolitical influences. The last dimension deals with specific skills (intervention techniques and strategies) needed in working with culturally different groups; it includes both individual and institutional competencies.

Dimension 1: Counselor Awareness of Own Assumptions, Values, and Biases

Culturally skilled counselors are actively in the process of becoming aware of their own assumptions about human behavior, values, biases, preconceived notions, personal limitations, and so forth. They understand their own worldviews, how they are products of their cultural conditioning, and how this may be reflected in their therapeutic work with culturally different groups. Counselor self-awareness is manifested in (a) beliefs and attitudes, (b) knowledge, and (c) skills. (The following is adapted from Sue, Arredondo & McDavis, 1992.)

Beliefs

1. Culturally skilled counselors have moved from being culturally unaware to being aware and sensitive to their own cultural heritage and to valuing and respecting differences.
2. Culturally skilled counselors are aware of how their own cultural background and experiences, attitudes, values, and biases influence psychological processes.
3. Culturally skilled counselors are able to recognize the limits of their competencies and expertise.
4. Culturally skilled counselors are comfortable with differences that exist between themselves and clients in race, ethnicity, culture, and beliefs.

Knowledge

1. Culturally skilled counselors have specific knowledge about their own racial and cultural heritage and how it personally and professionally affects their definitions and biases of normality-abnormality and the process of counseling.
2. Culturally skilled counselors possess knowledge and understanding about how oppression, racism, discrimination, and stereotyping affect them personally and in their work. This allows them to acknowledge their own racist attitudes, beliefs, and feelings. Although this standard applies to all groups, for White counselors it may mean that they understand how they may have

directly or indirectly benefited from individual, institutional, and cultural racism (White identity development models).

3. Culturally skilled counselors possess knowledge about their social impact on others. They are knowledgeable about communication style differences, how their style may clash or facilitate the counseling process with minority clients, and how to anticipate the impact it may have on others.

Skills

1. Culturally skilled counselors seek out educational, consultative, and training experiences to enrich their understanding and effectiveness in working with culturally different populations. Being able to recognize the limits of their competencies, they (a) seek consultation, (b) seek further training or education, (c) refer out to more qualified individuals or resources, or (d) engage in a combination of these.

2. Culturally skilled counselors are constantly seeking to understand themselves as racial and cultural beings and are actively seeking a nonracist identity.

Dimension 2: Understanding the Worldview of the Culturally Different Client

Culturally skilled counselors actively attempt to understand the worldview of their culturally different clients without negative judgments. It is crucial that counselors understand and share with respect and appreciation the worldviews of their culturally different clients. This does not imply that counselors have to hold the worldviews of their clients, but that they can accept them as another legitimate perspective.

Beliefs and Attitudes

1. Culturally skilled counselors are aware of their negative emotional reactions toward other racial and ethnic groups; these reactions may prove detrimental to their clients in counseling. They are willing to contrast their own beliefs and attitudes with those of their culturally different clients in a nonjudgmental fashion.

2. Culturally skilled counselors are aware of the stereotypes and preconceived notions that they may hold toward other racial and ethnic minority groups.

Knowledge

1. Culturally skilled counselors possess specific knowledge and information about the particular group with which they are working. They are aware of the life experiences, cultural heritage, and historical background of their

culturally different clients. This particular competency is strongly linked to the "minority identity development models" available in the literature.

2. Culturally skilled counselors understand how race, culture, ethnicity, and so forth may affect personality formation, vocational choices, manifestation of psychological disorders, help-seeking behavior, and the appropriateness or inappropriateness of counseling approaches.

3. Culturally skilled counselors understand and have knowledge about socio-political influences that impinge on the life of racial and ethnic minorities. Immigration issues, poverty, racism, stereotyping, and powerlessness all leave major scars that may influence the counseling process.

Skills

1. Culturally skilled counselors should familiarize themselves with relevant research and the latest findings regarding mental health and mental disorders of various ethnic and racial groups. They should actively seek out educational experiences that enrich their knowledge, understanding, and cross-cultural skills.

2. Culturally skilled counselors become actively involved with minority individuals outside the counseling setting (community events, social and political functions, celebrations, friendships, neighborhood groups, and so forth) so that their perspective of minorities is more than an academic or helping exercise.

Dimension 3: Developing Appropriate
Intervention Strategies and Techniques

Culturally skilled counselors are in the process of actively developing and practicing appropriate, relevant, and sensitive intervention strategies and skills in working with their culturally different clients. Studies consistently reveal that counseling effectiveness is improved when counselors use modalities and define goals consistent with the life experiences and cultural values of clients.

Attitudes and Beliefs

1. Culturally skilled counselors respect clients' religious beliefs and values, spiritual beliefs and values, or both about physical and mental functioning.

2. Culturally skilled counselors respect indigenous helping practices and respect minority community intrinsic help-giving networks.

3. Culturally skilled counselors value bilingualism and do not view another language as an impediment to counseling (monolingualism may be the culprit).

Knowledge

1. Culturally skilled counselors have a clear and explicit knowledge and understanding of the generic characteristics of counseling and therapy (culture bound, class bound, and monolingual) and how they may clash with the cultural values of various minority groups.
2. Culturally skilled counselors are aware of institutional barriers that prevent minorities from using mental health services.
3. Culturally skilled counselors have knowledge of the potential bias in assessment instruments and use procedures and interpret findings keeping in mind the cultural and linguistic characteristics of clients.
4. Culturally skilled counselors have knowledge of minority family structures, hierarchies, values, and beliefs. They are knowledgeable about the community characteristics and the resources in the community as well as the family.
5. Culturally skilled counselors should be aware of relevant discriminatory practices at the social and the community level that may be affecting the psychological welfare of the population being served.
6. *The culturally skilled psychologist or counselor has knowledge of models of minority and majority identity, and understands how these models relate to the counseling relationship and the counseling process.* (New added competency; see Chapter 6).

Skills

1. Culturally skilled counselors are able to engage in a variety of verbal and nonverbal helping responses. They are able to send and receive both verbal and nonverbal messages accurately and appropriately. They are not tied down to only one method or approach to helping but recognize that helping styles and approaches may be culture bound. When they sense that their helping style is limited and potentially inappropriate, they can anticipate and ameliorate its negative impact.
2. Culturally skilled counselors are able to exercise institutional intervention skills on behalf of their clients. They can help clients determine whether a "problem" stems from racism or bias in others (the concept of healthy paranoia), so that clients do not inappropriately blame themselves.
3. Culturally skilled counselors are not averse to seeking consultation with traditional healers or religious and spiritual leaders and practitioners in the treatment of culturally different clients when appropriate.
4. Culturally skilled counselors take responsibility for interacting in the language requested by the client; this may mean appropriate referral to outside resources. A serious problem arises when the linguistic skills of the counselor do not match the language of the client. This being the case, counselors should (a) seek a translator with cultural knowledge and appropriate professional background or (b) refer to a knowledgeable and competent bilingual counselor.

5. Culturally skilled counselors have training and expertise in the use of traditional assessment and testing instruments. They not only understand the technical aspects of the instruments but are also aware of the cultural limitations. This allows them to use test instruments for the welfare of the diverse clients.

6. Culturally skilled counselors should attend to as well as work to eliminate biases, prejudices, and discriminatory practices. They should be cognizant of sociopolitical contexts in conducting evaluations and providing interventions, and should develop sensitivity to issues of oppression, sexism, and racism.

7. Culturally skilled counselors take responsibility for educating their clients to the processes of psychological intervention such as goals, expectations, legal rights, and the counselor's orientation.

8. *The culturally skilled psychologist or counselor can tailor his or her relationship building strategies, intervention plans, and referral considerations to the particular stage of identity development of the client, while taking into account his or her own level of racial identity development.* (New competency added; see Chapter 6).

9. *Culturally skilled counselors are able to engage in psychoeducational or systems intervention roles, in addition to their clinical ones. Although the conventional counseling and clinical roles are valuable, other roles such as the consultant, advocate, adviser, teacher, facilitator of indigenous healing, and so on may prove more culturally appropriate.* (New competency added; see Chapter 7).

Adapted and reprinted from *Multicultural Counseling and Standards: A Call to the Profession, 70,* 1992, pp. 482-483. Reprinted with permission. No further reproduction authorized without written permission of the American Counseling Association.

Multicultural Organizational Competence

Although the focus of multicultural competence has been primarily directed at an individual level, organizations can also be seen as larger systems, which need to become multicultural as well. The diversification of the United States has had a tremendous impact on our economic, social, legal, political, educational, and cultural systems. Whereas our society is the most culturally diverse in the world, our organizations continue to be parochial and ethnocentric. Organizational entities that fail to successfully implement diversity into the very structures of their practice will fail to be relevant to their constituencies, and will fail to compete and survive.

Such a statement applies to all levels and types of organizations: (a) The mental health field must begin to alter the nature of education and training to recognize cultural diversity. It must also begin to change the nature of mental health delivery systems to make them more appropriate for a culturally diverse population. (b) Business and industry must begin to incorporate diversity into the workforce not only to successfully manage its multitude of workers, but also to recognize that the consumer of its goods and services will increasingly be racial/ethnic minorities. (c) Educational institutions are undergoing turmoil in the movement toward multicultural education. What implications does such a movement have for curriculum development, teaching styles/learning styles, campus climate, support systems, and so on? (d) Our professional organizations (American Psychological Association, American Business Association, American Counseling Association, National Educational Association, and so on) may currently function from monocultural standards of professional practice and ethics. As such, how do we move them toward a more multicultural stance?

Characteristics of a Culturally Competent Organization

The rationale and detailed characteristics of a multiculturally competent organization will be further developed in another chapter. In this section, however, we would like to outline some characteristics/conditions that seem to define culturally inclusive organizations. To begin this process, we use the definition developed by Barr and Strong (1987):

A multicultural organization is

- genuinely committed (action as well as words) to diverse representation throughout its organization and at all levels;
- sensitive to maintaining an open, supportive, and responsive environment;
- working toward and purposefully including elements of diverse cultures in its ongoing operations (organizational policies and practices are carefully monitored to the goals of multiculturalism);
- authentic in responding to issues confronting it (commitment to changing policies and practices that block cultural diversity).

Operationalizing this definition produces the following characteristics.

1. Culturally competent and inclusive organizations are ones that evidence multicultural commitment from the very top levels. Diversity implementation is most effective when strong leadership is exerted on behalf of

multiculturalism. Employees and members are most likely to watch the actions (not just words) of those in leadership positions. For higher education, it may be the provost, chancellor, president, dean, or chair of the department. In mental health delivery systems, it may be the director and program supervisors. For public schools, it may be the board of education, superintendent, and principals. For professional associations, it may be the executive director, president, council of representatives, and so forth. For business and industry, it may be the CEO, board of directors, department heads, or upper management.

2. Culturally competent and inclusive organizations have a written policy, mission or vision statement that frames the concepts of multiculturalism and diversity into a meaningful operational definition. This allows an organization to monitor its progress toward becoming more multicultural. The multicultural statement cannot be simply an "add on" but must be stated in such a manner as to infuse the concepts throughout an organization's operations, structures, and policies. Otherwise, such statements serve only as a cosmetic feature.

3. Culturally competent and inclusive organizations have developed a multicultural and diversity action plan with clear objectives and time lines. The existence of multicultural units or committees for discussion and exploration is not enough unless expected actions are the outcome. Too often organizations spend an inordinate amount of time identifying barriers and misunderstandings and attempt to create greater sensitivity among employees, students, mental health professionals, and so on. Although important and needed, meaningful change is often thwarted by concentrating solely on individual rather than systemic evolution. Thus, organizations must develop action plans that directly outline specific time frames for implementation of multicultural goals.

4. Culturally competent and inclusive organizations have created a superordinate or oversight team/group, which is empowered to assess, develop, and monitor the organization's development with respect to the goals of multiculturalism. Such groups have the power to operate rather independently, share an equal status relationship with other units in the organization, or both. Too often organizations are well intentioned in forming multicultural committees or groups that serve more in an advisory or educational capacity. Although somewhat helpful, such a group may lack the ability to influence, formulate, and implement multicultural initiatives because decision-making power resides at another or higher level of authority.

5. Culturally competent and inclusive organizations actively solicit feedback from employees related to issues of race, culture, gender, ethnicity, sexual orientation, and so forth. Feedback from employee groups provides a rich source of information (work climate issues, corporate policies and practices, and so on), which organizations may find useful in their movement toward valuing multiculturalism. They may sanction employee advocacy, focus,

and advisory groups. Such organizations send a strong message to their workers and consumers about the importance they place on identifying their needs and concerns; it also is a powerful statement of organizational inclusion.

6. Culturally competent and inclusive organizations build multicultural accountability into the system. Certain divisions, departments, and individuals must be held responsible for achieving the goals of diversity and multiculturalism. For example, upper management in business or deans and chairs of institutions of higher education might be held responsible for recruiting, retaining, and promoting minorities and women within their own units. Professors might be held accountable for incorporating diversity into their curriculum, recognizing the need for alternative teaching styles, and being unafraid to address topics likely to create difficult dialogues in the classroom (race, gender, sexual orientation, and so on).

7. Culturally competent and inclusive organizations infuse multiculturalism into evaluation criteria used for hiring and promotion of employees. If an organization values multicultural competencies, it must be built into the performance appraisal systems. For example, promotion and tenure criteria at a university considers good teaching to entail knowledge, sensitivities, and skills related to cross-cultural competence in all courses taught, not just those designated as "cultural" in nature. By incorporating multicultural competence into performance evaluations, the issue of race and gender would be minimized because Euro-Americans with multicultural competence would also be valued.

8. Culturally competent and inclusive organizations recognize that mentoring and support networks for minority employees are vital for success and that the presence of an "old boy's network" may adversely impact them. In the past, it was predominantly White males who enjoyed both formal and informal mentoring and support networks that either shut out minorities and women, or did little to provide them with such important help. Many nontraditional employees are unfamiliar with the corporate culture, the invisible and hidden rules and regulations that play a vital role in success, and the need to network with employees and superiors. This keeps minorities and women at the "lower levels" of an organization and blocks multicultural change.

9. Culturally competent and inclusive organizations encourage coalition building and networking among minorities and women. They are not threatened by "clustering" of employees along racial, cultural, or ethnic lines. They recognize that being a culturally different individual in a primarily monocultural work situation can deplete the energy of, alienate, and discourage the minority employee—thereby reducing work productivity. Clustering that allows for support and nourishment may ultimately lead to greater cross-cultural interactions in the long term.

10. Culturally competent and inclusive organizations have a systematic and long-term commitment to educate the entire workforce concerning diversity issues, to address barriers that block multiculturalism, and to increase the sensitivity of workers. Inservice multicultural training should be an intimate part of the organizations activities. This includes not only employees at the lower levels of employment, but should include the entire workforce up through the management team, to the senior executives and the CEO or president. Likewise, in higher education, it is not simply the faculty that needs multicultural training, but administrators as well.

11. Culturally competent and inclusive organizations are viewed as both part of and a reflection of the wider community. No organization exists apart from the wider community or society. Community linkages are very important to aid in the recruitment, retention, and promotion of minority employees.

Individual, professional, and institutional multicultural competence are the central keys to providing equal access and opportunity for all groups. The next five chapters have been keyed to the four major areas of multicultural competence: (a) awareness of one's own worldview (Chapter 5), (b) awareness of the worldview of the culturally different client (Chapter 6), (c) use of culturally appropriate intervention strategies (Chapter 7), and (d) developing multicultural organizations (Chapters 8 and 9). For several reasons, the frame of reference regarding "awareness of one's own worldview" is that of Euro-Americans. First, helping professionals and those in positions to affect mental health policy and practice continue to be predominantly White. Second, most theories of counseling and psychotherapy are primarily Euro-American in origin (Sue, Ivey, & Pedersen, 1996). Third, White culture is such an invisible veil for those socialized in this society (including persons of color) that it requires especially careful scrutiny. We recognize, however, that when therapists are persons of color, they, too, must be equally cognizant of their values, assumptions, and biases.

5

Understanding the Euro-American Worldview

MULTICULTURAL COUNSELING COMPETENCE IS . . .

- Being conversant and familiar with the major models of White racial identity/consciousness development.
- Understanding the process of White racial identity, the characteristics of the stages or the ego statuses and their implications for practice, education, and training.
- Knowing that the ultimate goal of healthy White development is related to

    Overthrowing the negative cultural conditioning of socialization

    Understanding self as a racial/cultural being

    Being aware of sociopolitical influences with respect to racism and how it affects intergroup relations

    Having an appreciation of racial/cultural diversity

    Increasing commitment toward eradicating oppression

A culturally skilled counselor is one who is actively in the process of becoming aware of his or her own assumptions about human behavior, values, biases, preconceived notions, personal limitations, and so forth. (Sue & Sue, 1990)

They understand their own worldviews, how they are the product of their cultural conditioning, and how it may be reflected in their counseling and work with racial and ethnic minorities. The old adage "counselor, know thyself" is important in not allowing biases, values, or "hang-ups" to interfere with the counselor's ability to work with clients. (Sue, Arredondo, & McDavis, 1992, p. 481)

Understanding one's own worldview (Euro-American) necessitates freeing ourselves from our cultural conditioning. Katz (1985) points out the difficulty in involving Whites in an investigation of their own cultural identity and worldview.

> Because White culture is the dominant cultural norm in the United States, it acts as an invisible veil that limits many people from seeing it as a cultural system. . . . Often, it is easier for many Whites to identify and acknowledge the different cultures of minorities than to accept their own racial identity. . . . The difficulty of accepting such a view is that White culture is omnipresent. It is so interwoven in the fabric of everyday living that Whites cannot step outside and see their beliefs, values, and behaviors as creating a distinct cultural group. (pp. 616-617)

Carter (1990) has noted that a common response by many organizations to racial tensions has been to offer antiracism training. Supporting the idea that racial/ethnic identity development should be addressed to both minority and majority individuals, Carter says "one shortcoming of antiracism training is that it does not explore differences in Whites' awareness of their status of racial beings . . . it seems important for counselors and educators to begin to consider how racist attitudes might be related to variations in White racial identity . . . Whites seldom have an opportunity to examine the meaning of their Whiteness" (p. 46). His preliminary research indicates that there may be complex interactions between gender, White racial identity attitudes, and racism (Carter, 1995).

Although the multicultural counseling standards allow us to define the culturally competent helping professional, the standards have been weaker in providing us with a model or theoretical basis for examining and ameliorating the biases, "blind spots," and misattributions that limit counseling effectiveness. Ridley and colleagues (Ridley, Mendoza, Kanitz, Angermeier, & Zenk, 1994) have proposed a perceptual schema model to explain cultural sensitivity. The perceptual schemas that counselors possess affect how information from the environment is collected, organized, and interpreted. When cultural differences exist between the counselor and client, the mental structures of the counselor may not only limit what information is processed, but may also distort the meaning of the data. Because our perceptual schemas are most likely products of cultural conditioning, it is these schemas that may reduce cultural sensitivity. According to Ridley et al. (1994), cultural sensitivity is "the ability of counselors to acquire, develop, and actively use an accurate cultural perceptual schema in the course of multicultural counseling."

Models of White Racial Identity/Consciousness Development

Within all the literature on multicultural counseling, growing attention has been paid to the study of individual racial/ethnic minority identity development. A number of investigators have extended their research to examine the relationship between a White Euro-American counselor's racial/ethnic identity, and his or her readiness for training in multicultural awareness, knowledge, and skills (Carney & Kahn, 1984; Helms, 1990; Ponterotto, 1988; Sabnani, Ponterotto, & Borodovsky, 1991; Sue & Sue, 1990). Because developing multicultural sensitivity is a long-term developmental task, the work of many researchers has gradually converged toward a conceptualization of the stages/levels of consciousness of racial/ethnic identity development for both minorities and Whites (Bennett, 1986; Smith, 1991). A number of these theories describe the salience of identity for establishing relationships between counselors and clients, and some have now linked stages of identity with stages for appropriate training (Bennett, 1986; Carney & Kahn, 1984; Sabnani et al., 1991).

Smith (1991) and many other authors cite the work of Cross (1971) as providing the earliest models of racial identity development, which dealt primarily with the issue of racial oppression and African Americans' identity development in relation to it. Smith is critical of the fact that much of the research has remained focused on racial identity awareness, rather than what she describes as the more generic concept of ethnic identity development. Ethnic identity development can apply to majority as well as minority groups, and does not limit the concept of identity development to reactions against an oppressive, racist society. Phinney and Rotheram (1987) advocate this universal application of ethnic identity, arguing that this way, "the distinctive characteristics of each group can be examined and understood in their own terms, rather than as deviations from the 'norm' of a dominant culture" (p. 12). They also acknowledge, however, that "when ethnicity and minority status co-occur, predictable social psychological processes occur both within the group and between the group and the majority culture" (p. 12). In this chapter, we will concentrate on understanding the White Euro-American worldview as it manifests itself in identity formation and its impact on multicultural development.

The Hardiman Model

Perhaps one of the earliest integrative attempts at formulating a White racial identity development model (WRID) is that of Hardiman (1982). Her model was formulated via a study of White antiracist activists. The autobiographies of these individuals, who she believed had attained a high level of racial consciousness, led to her identification of five White developmental stages: (a) Naivete, (b) Acceptance, (c) Resistance, (d) Redefinition, and (e) Internalization.

The *Naivete* stage is characteristic of "early childhood" when we are born into this world innocent, open, unaware of racism and the importance of race. There is little discomfort associated with race or racial differences, bias and prejudice are either absent or minimal, and the youngster tends to be spontaneous and curious when he or she notices differences. Such an orientation becomes less characteristic of the child as the socialization process progresses. Parents, relatives, friends, peers, the educational system, and mass media exert a tremendous influence on the child. Values, belief systems, bias, and stereotypes become progressively inculcated into the child as he or she moves into the Acceptance stage.

The *Acceptance* stage is characterized by the acquisition of many appropriate values, beliefs, and skills, but it also means increasing belief in and a conscious and unconscious support of White superiority and White privilege. Likewise, there is belief in the inferiority of minority groups, that all groups have an equal opportunity in the society, and that those who fail must bear the responsibility for their failure. Although there may be awareness of one's Whiteness, racial issues are usually rationalized to fit the basic assumption of White supremacy. The existence of oppression is denied, and denial of differences is used as a means for not seeing oppression.

Over time, assumptions of White superiority and the denial of racism and discrimination begin to be challenged. This is a very uncomfortable and painful transition point—moving from the Acceptance to the *Resistance* stage. The racial realities of life in the United States can no longer be denied. The change from one stage to another might take considerable time, but once completed, the person becomes conscious of being White, is aware that he or she harbors racist attitudes, and begins to see the pervasiveness of oppression in our society. Feelings of anger, pain, hurt, rage, and frustration are present. The person may begin to "look down" on or become angry with Whites and the White world. Although these individuals may romanticize people of color, they cannot interact confidently with them because they fear making racist mistakes. According to Hardiman (1982), the person becomes motivated to ask the question "Who am

I?" There is discomfort with existing in limbo or on the margins of rejecting one's Whiteness and realizing that one is White.

When this process swings into action, the person enters the *Redefinition* stage. New ways of defining their social group and their membership in that group become important. There is a realization that Whiteness has been defined in opposition to people of color—by standards of White supremacy. Stepping out of this racist paradigm and redefining what his or her Whiteness means adds meaning to one's nonracist identity. The extremes of good/bad or positive/negative attachments to "White" and "people of color" begin to become more realistic. The person no longer denies being White, honestly confronts one's racism, understands the concept of White privilege, and feels increased comfort in relating to persons of color.

The *Internalization* stage is the result of forming a new social and personal identity. The racist-free identity, however, must be nurtured, validated, and supported to be sustained in a hostile environment. Such an individual is constantly bombarded by attempts to be resocialized into the oppressive society.

The Hardiman model has several limitations. First, the select and limited sample from which she derives the stages and enumerates the characteristics makes potential generalization of the findings suspect. The autobiographies of White Americans may not be truly representative and their experiences with racism may be bound by the era of the times. Second, the stages are tied to existing social identity development theories and the model proposes a Naivete stage that, for all practical purposes, exists only in children (4 to 5 years of age). It seems to only have a tangential place in the model and might better be conceptualized as part of the Acceptance stage of socialization. Third, to date, no direct empirical or other postmodern methods of exploration concerning the model has occurred. Despite these cautions and potential limitations, Hardiman (1982) has contributed greatly to our understanding of White identity development by focusing attention on racism as a central force in the socialization of White Americans.

The Helms Model

Like Hardiman, Helms's White racial identity model (Helms, 1984, 1990, 1994a, 1995) assumes that racism is an intimate and central part of being a White American. Perhaps the most influential White identity development theorist, Helms conceptualizes a general two-phase process (Phase 1: Abandonment of Racism and Phase 2: Defining a Nonracist

White Identity) with six specific racial identity statuses equally distributed in the two: Contact, Disintegration, Reintegration, Pseudo-Independence, Immersion/Emersion, and Autonomy. These statuses were originally termed "stages," but due to certain conceptual ambiguities and the controversy that ensued, Helms has abandoned its usage.

1. *Contact:* People in this status are oblivious to racism, lack an understanding of racism, have minimal experiences with Black people, and may profess to be color-blind. Societal influence in perpetuating stereotypes and the superior/inferior dichotomy associated between Blacks and Whites are not noticed, but accepted unconsciously or consciously without critical thought or analysis. Racial and cultural differences are considered unimportant and these individuals seldom perceive themselves as "dominant" group members, or having biases and prejudices.

2. *Disintegration:* In this state, the person becomes conflicted over unresolvable racial moral dilemmas that are frequently perceived as polar opposites: believing one is nonracist, yet not wanting one's son or daughter to marry a minority group member; believing that "all men are created equal," yet society treating Blacks as second class citizens; and not acknowledging that oppression exists while witnessing it (à la the beating of Rodney King in Los Angeles). The person becomes increasingly conscious of his or her Whiteness and may experience dissonance and conflict between choosing between own-group loyalty and humanism.

3. *Reintegration:* Because of the tremendous influence that societal ideology exerts, initial resolution of dissonance often moves in the direction of the dominant ideology associated with race and one's own socioracial group identity. This stage may be characterized as a regression, for the tendency is to idealize one's socioracial group and to be intolerant of other minority groups. There is a firmer and more conscious belief in White racial superiority and racial/ethnic minorities are blamed for their own problems.

4. *Pseudo-Independence:* A person is likely to move into this phase due to a painful or insightful encounter or event, which jars the person from Reintegration status. The person begins to attempt an understanding of racial, cultural, and sexual orientation differences and may reach out to interact with minority group members. The choice of minority individuals, however, is based on how "similar" they are to him or her, and the primary mechanism used to understand racial issues is intellectual and conceptual. An attempt to understand has not reached the experiential and affective domains. In other words, understanding Euro-American White privilege, the sociopolitical aspects of race, and issues of bias, prejudice, and discrimination tend to be more an intellectual exercise.

5. *Immersion/Emersion*: If the person is reinforced to continue a personal exploration of himself or herself as a racial being, questions become focused

on what it means to be White. Helms states that the person searches for an understanding of the personal meaning of racism and the ways by which one benefits from White privilege. There is an increasing willingness to truly confront one's own biases, to redefine Whiteness, and to become more activistic in directly combating racism and oppression. This stage is marked with increasing experiential and affective understanding that were lacking in the previous status.

6. *Autonomy:* Increasing awareness of one's own Whiteness, reduced feelings of guilt, acceptance of one's role in perpetuating racism, and renewed determination to abandon White entitlement leads to an autonomy status. The person is knowledgeable about racial, ethnic, and cultural differences, values the diversity, and is no longer fearful, intimidated, or uncomfortable with the experiential reality of race. Development of a nonracist White identity becomes increasingly strong.

Helms's model is by far the most widely cited, researched, and applied of all the White racial identity formulations. Part of its attractiveness and value is the derivation of "defenses," "protective strategies," or what Helms (1995) formally labels *information-processing strategies* (IPS), which White people use to avoid or assuage anxiety and discomfort around the issue of race. Each status has a dominant IPS associated with it: Contact = obliviousness or denial, Disintegration = suppression and ambivalence, Reintegration = selective perception and negative out-group distortion, Pseudo-independence = reshaping reality and selective perception, Immersion/emersion = hypervigilance and reshaping, and Autonomy = flexibility and complexity. Understanding these strategic reactions is important for White American identity development, for understanding the barriers that must be overcome to move to another status, and for potentially developing effective training or clinical strategies.

The Helms's model, however, is not without its detractors. In an article critical of Helms's model and of most "stage" models of White racial identity development, Rowe, Bennett, and Atkinson (1994) raise some serious objections. First, they claim Helms's WRID model to be erroneously based on racial/ethnic minority identity development models (to be discussed in the next chapter). Because minority identity development occurs in the face of stereotyping and oppression, they may be inapplicable to White identity, which does not occur under similar conditions. Second, they believe too much emphasis is placed on the development of White attitudes toward minorities and not enough on the development of White attitudes toward themselves and their own identity. Third, they claim that there is a conceptual inaccuracy in putting forth the model as developmental via stages (linear) and that the progression from less to more healthy seems based on the creators' ethics.

It is important to note that the critique of Helms (1984) model has not been left unanswered. Thompson (1995) believes that these criticisms are based on a misrepresentation of Helms's writings and research—that she does emphasize White identity and minority identity development in different contexts, that the task of developing a positive White identity is central to the model, and that the model does meet criteria for a developmental theory that is not necessarily linear. Helms (1994, 1995), in subsequent writings, has also disclaimed the Rowe et al. (1994) characterization of her model and has attempted to clarify her position.

The continuing debate has proven beneficial for two reasons. First, the Helms's model has evolved and changed (whether because of these criticism or not) so that it has become even more intricate and clear. For example, Helms (1995) disclaims ever being a "stage theorist," but to prevent continuing future confusion, she now prefers the term "status" and describes her thinking on this issue in detail. Second, in responding to the Helms's model, Rowe et al. (1994) offer an alternative means of conceptualizing White identity, which has contributed to the increasing understanding of WRID. Let us briefly describe their model.

Rowe, Bennett, and Atkinson's White Racial Consciousness Model

Taking issue with the Helms model, Rowe et al. (1994) prefer to conceptualize White racial identity as one of "types" or "statuses" rather than "stages." They take care in explaining that these types are not fixed entities but subject to experiential modification. They propose two major groupings with seven types of racial consciousness: Unachieved (avoidant, dependent, and dissonant) and Achieved (dominative, conflictive, reactive, and integrative).

Unachieved

- *Avoidant* types ignore, avoid, deny, or minimize racial issues. They do not consider their own racial identity nor are they seemingly aware of minority issues.
- *Dependent* types have minimal racial attitudes developed through personal experience or consideration. They most often follow the lead of significant others in their lives, such as a child would with his or her parent.
- *Dissonant* types often feel conflict between their belief system and contradictory experiences. This type may break away from these attitudes depend-

ing on the degree of support or the intensity of the conflict. As such, it is a transitory status for the person.

Achieved

- *Dominative* types are very ethnocentric, believe in White superiority and minority inferiority. They may passively act out their biases or actively do so.
- *Conflictive* types oppose direct and obvious discrimination, but would be unwilling to change the status quo. Most feel that discrimination has been eliminated and further efforts constitute reverse racism.
- *Reactive* types have a good awareness that racism exists but seem unaware of their personal responsibility in perpetuating it. They may overidentify with or are paternal toward minorities.
- *Integrative* types "have integrated their sense of Whiteness with a regard for racial/ethnic minorities . . (and) integrate rational analysis, on one hand, and moral principles, on the other, as they relate to a variety of racial/ethnic issues" (Rowe et al., 1994, p. 141).

Movement from type to type is dependent on the creation of "dissonance," personal attributes, and the subsequent environmental conditions encountered by the person. As a result, the primary gateway for change involves the dissonant type. Persons can move between all types except the two unachieved ones—avoidant and dependent. These latter two are characterized by lack of internalized attitudes.

The Process of White Racial Identity Development: A Descriptive Model

Analysis of the models proposed by Hardiman; Helms; and Rowe, Bennett, and Atkinson reveals some important differences. First, the identity development models seem to focus on a more definite and sequential movement through stages or statuses. They differ, however, in where they place the particular stages or statuses in the developmental process. Given that almost all models now entertain the possibility that development can vary (looping and recycling), the consciousness development models allows greater latitude conceptually for movement to various types. They seem to offer a more fluid process of racial experience by White people. Because of this factor, these models are also less bound by the context or era of the times (identity formed during the civil rights movement vs. current time). The addition of Nonachieved statuses is something missing in the development theories and may capture more closely the "passive" feel that White folks experience in their racial identity development.

Yet, the essential concept of developing a positive White identity is conspicuously absent from the consciousness models. It does not allow Whites to explain or view their developmental history better, or to gain a sense of their past, the present, or their future direction. Struggling with racial identity and the issues of race requires a historical perspective that development theories offer. It is with this in mind that we have taken aspects of White racial identity/consciousness development in formulating a descriptive model with practice implications.

Using the formulation of Sue and Sue (1990), we propose a five-stage process whereby many of the characteristics from the other formulations are integrated. We furthermore make some basic assumptions with respect to those models: (a) Racism is an integral part of U.S. life and permeates all aspects of our culture and institutions (ethnocentric monoculturalism); (b) Whites are socialized into the society and therefore inherit all the biases, stereotypes, and racist attitudes, beliefs, and behaviors of the larger society; (c) how Whites perceive themselves as racial beings follows an identifiable sequence that can occur in a linear or nonlinear fashion; (d) the status of White racial identity development in any multicultural encounter affects the process and outcome of interracial relationships; and (e) the most desirable outcome is one in which the White person not only accepts his or her Whiteness, but also defines it in a nondefensive and nonracist manner.

1. *Conformity:* The White person's beliefs and attitudes in this phase are very ethnocentric and there is minimal awareness of self as a racial/cultural being. Individuals are likely to have little knowledge or understanding of other culturally different groups; they derive most of their knowledge from stereotypes and images portrayed by the mass media or from misconceptions passed on from family and friends. Like a fish in water, Whites have difficulty or are unable to see the invisible veil of cultural assumptions, biases, and prejudices that guide their perceptions and actions. They tend to believe that White Euro-American culture is superior and that other cultures are primitive, inferior, less developed, or lower on the scale of evolution. It is important to note that many Whites in this phase of development are unaware of these beliefs and operate as if they are universally shared by others. They believe that differences are unimportant and that "people are people," "we are all the same under the skin," "we should treat everyone the same," "problems wouldn't exist if minorities would only assimilate," and that discrimination and prejudice are things that others do. The helping professional with this perspective professes

"color blindness" and views counseling/therapy theories as universally applicable and does not question their relevance to other culturally different groups.

Wrenn's (1962, 1985) reference and description of the "culturally encapsulated counselor" fulfills characteristics of conformity. The primary mechanism used in encapsulation is denial—denial that people are different, denial that discrimination exists, and denial of one's own prejudices. Instead, the locus of the problem is seen to reside in the minority individual or group. Minorities would not encounter problems if they would assimilate and acculturate (melting pot), if they would value education, or if they would only work harder.

2. *Dissonance:* Dissonance is created in the White person when information or experience become inconsistent with a previously held belief or attitude. For example, a person who may consciously believe that "all men are created equal" and that he or she "treats everyone the same" suddenly experiences reservations about having African Americans move next door or having their son or daughter involved in an interracial relationship. These more personal experiences bring the individual face to face with his or her own prejudices and biases. In this situation, thoughts that "I am not prejudiced," "I treat everyone the same regardless of race, creed, or color," and "I do not discriminate" collide with the denial system. Or, some major event (the assassination of Martin Luther King, viewing the Rodney King beating, and so on) may force the person to realize that "racism is alive and well in the United States."

The increasing realization that one is biased and that Euro-American society does play a part in oppressing minority groups is an unpleasant one. Dissonance may result in feelings of guilt, shame, anger, and depression. Rationalizations may become the manner used to exonerate one's own inactivity in combating perceived injustice or personal feelings of prejudice: "I'm only one person, what can I do?" or "Everyone is prejudiced, even minorities." As these conflicts ensue, the White person may retreat into the protective confines of White culture (encapsulation of the previous stage) or move progressively toward insight and revelation (resistance and immersion stage). Whether a person retreats or moves forward depends on a number of factors. Primary among them may be negative or positive social/environmental conditions. If friends and relatives express strong attitudes and beliefs of the conformity stage and the person fears potential ostracism or loss of social support, he or she may move backwards. If, however, others (may include some family and friends) are more accepting, forward movement is more likely.

3. *Resistance and Immersion:* This phase of development is marked by a major questioning of one's own racism and that of others in society. In addition, increasing awareness of how racism operates and its pervasiveness in U.S. culture and institutions are the major hallmark at this level. It is as if the person has awakened to the realities of oppression; sees how educational materials, the mass media, advertising, and so on portray and perpetuate stereotypes; and recognizes how being White has allowed him or her certain advantages denied to various minority groups.

At this level of development, the White person is likely to experience two contrasting feelings: anger at having been sold a false bill of goods by family, friends, and society, and guilt for having been a part of the oppressive system. In many ways, there is a strong realization that he or she has been a part of the problem and has participated (knowingly or unknowingly) in the oppression of others. A common reaction may be "racial self-hatred" where the person feels ashamed of his or her "Whiteness" and may try to consciously or unconsciously disown it. Because of the association of oppression with Whiteness, the person may unconsciously take on the roles of "paternalistic protector" or "overidentification with a minority group" (Helms, 1984; Ponterotto, 1988). In the former, the person often acts as an extremist White liberal, who frequently champions the causes of minority groups, who constantly speaks on their behalf, and who sees racism everywhere. In the latter, the person wants to reject their own Whiteness so strongly that they may actually desire to adopt the ways of a particular minority group (the person may seek out only from members of the minority group, attend only their functions, and seek validation from that group). It is important to note that most minority group members may find these roles not only paternalistic, but also an indication of "White guilt."

4. *Introspective:* This phase is most likely a compromise of having swung from an extreme of unconditional acceptance of White identity to a rejection of Whiteness. It is a state of relative quiescence, introspection, and reformulation of what it means to be White. These people realize and no longer deny that they have participated in oppression, that they benefit from White privilege, and that racism is an integral part of U.S. society. They, however, become less motivated by guilt and defensiveness, accept their Whiteness, and seek to define their own identity and that of their social group. This acceptance, however, does not mean a less active role in combating oppression. The process may involve addressing the questions: "What does it mean to be White?" "Who am I in relation to my Whiteness?" "Who am I as a racial/cultural being?"

The feelings or affective elements may be existential in nature and involve feelings of lack of connectedness, isolation, confusion, and loss. In other words, these people know that they will never fully understand the "minority experience" but feels disconnected from their Euro-American group as well. In some ways, the introspective phase is similar in dynamics to the dissonance phase in that both represent a transition from one perspective to another. The process used to answer the previous questions and to deal with the ensuing feelings may involve a searching, observing, and questioning attitude. Answers to these questions involve dialoguing and observing one's own social group and actively creating and experiencing interactions with various minority group members as well.

5. *Integrative awareness:* Reaching this level of development is most characterized as (a) understanding self as a racial/cultural being, (b) awareness of sociopolitical influences with respect to racism, (c) appreciation of racial/cultural diversity, and (d) increased commitment toward eradicating oppression. The formation of a nonracist White Euro-American identity emerges and becomes internalized. The person values multiculturalism, is comfortable around members of culturally different groups, and feels a strong connectedness with members of many groups. Perhaps, most important, is the inner sense of security and strength that needs to develop and that is needed to function in a society that is only marginally accepting of integratively aware White persons.

Implications for Multicultural Competence

If we acknowledge, as suggested by WRID theorists, that becoming aware of one's own White identity is an important attribute of multicultural competence, then it means several important things in the helping professions. Counseling and clinical training programs, for example, would be advised to assess the phase of development for White trainees with respect to WRID. The characteristics associated with one level may dictate the types of objectives and techniques most successful in use with trainees. Linking specific stages of development with ideas for training, Carney and Kahn (1984) described a five-stage counselor development model that applied to counselor trainees who, although not explicitly described as such, are taken to be White. They identified appropriate learning environment features related to each unnamed stage of counselor development, and discussed points at which it might be important to use same-culture, mixed culture, and other-culture trainers.

The work of Ponterotto and his colleagues (Ponterotto, 1988; Sabnani, Ponterotto, & Borodovsky, 1991) has focused on integrating general models of White racial identity into a developmental training model specifically designed for White counselors. Sabnani et al. (1991) have integrated and collapsed the models of Hardiman (1982), Helms (1984), and Ponterotto (1988) into a five-stage developmental model. Stage 1, Preexposure/ Precontact, is characterized by a general lack of awareness of self as a racial being. In Stage 2, Conflict, there is an expansion of knowledge regarding racial matters incurred through interactions with non-White persons or through exposure during training (e.g., a required multicultural course). This stage is characterized by conflict between the desire to conform to majority-group norms, while at the same time wishing to represent humanistic, nonracist values. The emotions of guilt, depression, and anger are common in this stage and result from the aforementioned conflict, and/or from an increasing awareness that racism continues in U.S. society.

In Stage 3, Prominority/Antiracism, the White individual develops a strong prominority stance concomitant with the rejection of internalized racist beliefs and anger directed at the White status quo. This affective reaction serves to alleviate the guilt common to Stage 2. Stage 4, Retreat Into White Culture, occurs when a White person perceives rejection from non-White persons or from the minority community. This retreat into the familiarity of same-race relations may also occur in response to a White person's lack of self-assuredness in interracial situations. Feelings of defensiveness, anger, and fear are associated with this stage. Finally, Stage 5, Redefinition and Integration, is characterized by a movement toward the clear development of White racial identity and a culturally transcendent worldview.

Emphasizing the developmental nature of their identity model and acknowledging that different majority-group counselors are at varied stages of readiness for incorporating multicultural training, Sabnani et al. (1991) outlined detailed and specific training exercises designed to facilitate movement through the stages. The authors organized their training regiments for each racial identity stage within the context of both training goals and tasks for each of the competency areas (Beliefs/Attitudes, Knowledge, and Skills) posited in the initial competency position paper (Sue et al., 1982).

Table 5.1 summarizes the stage-specific training exercises. This table is reprinted from Sabnani et al. (1991) and has been modified only by adding a final column specifying when and how each of the original 11 cross-cultural competencies (Sue et al., 1982) are met.

(text continued on page 65)

Table 5.1 Cross-Cultural Counseling Training Goals and Tasks

Stage	Beliefs/Attitudes Goals	Beliefs/Attitudes Tasks	Knowledge Goals	Knowledge Tasks	Skills Goals	Skills Tasks	For additional information see Sue et al., 1982 (Competencies Met)
1. Preexposure/ Precontact	Awareness of one's own cultural heritage Awareness of the cultural heritage of minority groups	Awareness group experience (McDavis & Parker, 1977; Parker & McDavis, 1979) "Ethnic dinners" (McDavis & Parker, 1977) Tours/exhibits of other cultures' crafts/areas Intercultural sharing (Parker, 1988) Multicultural action planning (low level of active involvement) (Parker, 1988) Free Drawing Test (Weeks et al., 1977) Public and private self-awareness exercise (Pedersen, 1988)	Knowledge of the cultural heritage of other minority groups	Research into the history of other cultures Intercultural sharing (Parker, 1988) Multicultural action planning (low level of active involvement) (Parker, 1988) Ethnic literature reviews Field trips Case studies (Pedersen, 1988) Culture assimilator (Albert, 1983; Brislin et al., 1986; Merta, Stringham, & Ponterotto, 1988)	Beginning development of counseling skills	Regular counselor training tasks (microskills training [Ivey & Authier, 1978; Egan, 1982; Carkhuff & Anthony, 1979])	*Beliefs/Attitudes* Competency 1 *Knowledge* Competency 2 Competency 3

continued

Table 5.1 continued

| Stage | Beliefs/Attitudes | | Knowledge | | Skills | | For additional information see Sue et al., 1982 |
	Goals	Tasks	Goals	Tasks	Goals	Tasks	(Competencies Met)
		Value statements exercise (Weeks et al., 1977) Decision awareness exercise (Pedersen, 1988)					
2. Conflict	Awareness of one's stereotypes and prejudicial attitudes and the impact of these on minorities Awareness of the conflict between wanting to conform to White norms while upholding humanitarian values Dealing with feelings of guilt and depression or anger	Critical incidents exercise (Weeks et al., 1977) Implicit assumptions checklist exercise (Weeks et al., 1977) We and you exercise (Weeks et al., 1977) Exercise for experiencing stereotypes (Parker, 1988) Stereotypes awareness exercise (Pedersen, 1988) Less structured cross-cultural encounter groups	More extensive knowledge of other cultures Knowledge of the concepts of prejudice and racism Knowledge of the impact of racism on minorities and the priviledges of being White	MAP—Investigative (Parker, 1988) Tours to other communities Research on racism in the past and present Classes in multicultural issues presenting survey data on minorities Films	Develop more client-specific methods of intervention	Critical incidents method (Sue, 1981) Role play exercise (Weeks et al., 1977) Role playing a problem in a group (Weeks et al., 1977)	*Beliefs/Attitudes* Competency 2 *Knowledge* Competency 1 Competency 2 Competency 4 *Skills* Competency 1 Competency 2 Competency 3

Stage	Awareness	Exercises	Knowledge	Development	Skills Training	Competencies
3. Prominority/ Antiracism	Awareness of over-identification and of paternalizing attitudes, and the impact of these on minorities.	Interracial encounters (Katz & Ivey, 1977) Cross-cultural encounter groups Responsible feedback exercise (Weeks et al., 1977) Anonymous feedback from the group exercise (Weeks et al., 1977)	Further immersion into other cultures	Guided self-study Exposure to audiovisual presentations (Pedersen, 1988) Interviews with consultants and experts (Pedersen, 1988) Lectures	Continue developing culturally emic and etic approaches to counseling Research into the impact of race on counseling	Role playing exercises Communication skills training Facilitating interracial groups (FIG) (McDavis & Parker, 1977) Counseling ethnic minorities (CEMI) (McDavis & Parker, 1977)	*Beliefs/Attitudes* Competency 3 Competency 4 *Knowledge* Competency 1 Competency 2 Competency 4 *Skills* Competency 1 Competency 2 Competency 3
4. Retreat into White Culture	Awareness of and dealing with one's own fear and anger	Cross-cultural encounter groups Lump sum (Weeks et al., 1977)	Knowledge of the development of minority identity and White identity	Research into minority identity development models Research into White identity development models	Building culturally etic (transcendent) approaches	Microskills training (Ponterotto and Benesch, 1988)	*Knowledge* Competency 2 Competency 3

continued

Table 5.1 continued

Stage	Beliefs/Attitudes Goals	Beliefs/Attitudes Tasks	Knowledge Goals	Knowledge Tasks	Skills Goals	Skills Tasks	For additional information see Sue et al., 1982 (Competencies Met)
5. Redefinition and integration	Develop an identity that claims Whiteness as a part of it	Feedback related exercises (see Stage 3)	Expand knowledge on racism in the real world	Visits to communities with large minority populations. Expand knowledge on counseling methods more appropriate to minorities	Deepen more culturally emic approaches. Face more challenging cross-cultural counseling interactions	Facilitating inter-racial groups (FIG) (McDavis & Parker, 1977) Counseling ethnic minorities individually (CEMI) (McDavis & Parker, 1977) Triad model (Pedersen 1988) Cross-cultural practices	*Beliefs/Attitudes* Competency 1 Competency 2 Competency 3 *Knowledge* Competency 1 Competency 2 Competency 3 Competency 4 Skills Competency 1 Competency 2 Competency 3 Competency 4

SOURCE: Adapted from Sabnani, Ponterotto, and Borodovsky (1991).

The Future of White or Euro-American Identity

The demographic evidence suggests that ethnic/cultural identities in the United States are likely to become more complex in the future, not only because of a continued influx of immigrants and refugees from around the world, but because of changing patterns in White ethnic identification (Alba, 1990). The significance of these changes are not entirely clear, but they may provide Whites with a new framework for identifying with culturally diverse groups—or they may provide more sophisticated ways for Whites to maintain various forms of institutional racism. This is why continued research that includes models of both majority and minority identity development are so important (Ponterotto, 1991).

Alba (1990) argues that ethnicity among Whites is in the midst of a fundamental transformation toward a more general identification as "European American," for several reasons. To the degree that most White Americans, who are generally several generations away from being immigrants, do identify with one or more particular ethnic groups, they appear to be choosing to maintain an ethnic identity as a way of describing family history, what Alba calls a "privatization of ethnic identity—a reduction of its expression to largely personal and family terms" (p. 300).

On the other hand, there are political forces providing incentives for Whites to define themselves in terms of ethnicity, rather than race. Describing his reasons for organizing a European American study group, one White activist said,

> We've left our chair at the multicultural table empty, and the multicultural table is where the debate is, where the deals are being made—about voting rights, immigrant services, immigration laws, redistricting, health policy. More and more, it's now being built around ethnicity.
>
> If European Americans aren't going to start speaking out of that ethnic voice, we are not engaged in the public discourse of our times.
>
> Americans are taught that European Americans are a monolithic group that look alike, act alike, come from a country called White Land and speak whitespeak. We would like to have our diversity respected. (Warner, as quoted in Ness, 1992, p. B4).

Alba (1990) suggests that all Americans are acquiring a perspective that now defines the American experience as that of immigration and its aftermath, rather than the earlier colonial and revolutionary experience. From this perspective, most Whites can claim the prototypical American heritage, as can almost any group except African Americans and American Indians. The immigrant history, highlighting the personal sacrifices of each family, is not ethnically exclusive, and allows almost anyone a moral claim to being an American. As the numerically dominant population group, however, European Americans get to define "the rules of the game" by which other groups must play if they are to lay claim to an American identity. Alba therefore cautions that although a White shift to a European American ethnic identity may facilitate the acceptance of multiculturalism, it may also provide Whites with just another way to claim differences, rather than similarities, with other groups.

If Whites are successful in shifting the terms of the debate away from examinations of actual power differences and forms of institutional discrimination, this may have serious effects on all systems, not just mental health and counseling organizations. Smith and Vasquez (1985) raise an interesting cautionary point, noting that increasing numbers of White researchers are writing about cross-cultural issues. It is possible that, ironically, this may limit the opportunities of minority researchers to publish or receive funding for work in this field, if institutional racism promotes White researchers ahead of minorities.

6

Understanding Racial/Ethnic
Minority Worldviews

MULTICULTURAL COUNSELING
COMPETENCE IS . . .

- Being conversant and familiar with the major models of minority racial/cultural identity development:

    Black racial identity development models

    Asian American identity development models

    Latino(a)/Hispanic identity development models

    Other identity development models related to gender, sexual orientation, and so on

- Understanding the characteristics and processes of the development stages or statuses with respect to practice, education, and training.

- Knowing that healthy minority identity development is related to

    Overcoming internalized racism

    Understanding self as a racial/cultural being

    Beingg aware of sociopolitical forces of oppression and how it affects intergroup relations

    Appreciating racial/cultural diversity

    Increasing commitment to social action

A culturally skilled counselor is one who actively attempts to understand the worldview of his or her culturally different client without negative judgments. It is crucial that counselors understand and share the worldviews of their culturally different clients with respect and appreciation. This statement does not imply that counselors have to hold the worldviews as their own, but can accept them as another legitimate perspective. . . . Culturally skilled counselors understand how race, culture, ethnicity, and so forth may affect personality formation vocational choices, manifestation of psychological disorders, help-seeking behavior, and the appropriateness or inappropriateness of counseling approaches. (Sue et al., 1991, pp. 481, 482).

These statements were made in reference to racial/ethnic minorities. It was suggested that one of the important attributes of becoming a culturally skilled counselor or therapist required racially and culturally based knowledge and understanding. It meant that helping professionals needed to consider racial/cultural differences (i.e., that they not profess to be color-blind) as an intimate determinant of identity and worldview.

The notion that minority individuals have varying racial and cultural levels of identity may be seen more clearly by way of racial and cultural models of identity development (Cross, 1978; Helms, 1984). Numerous models exist in the literature. A few will be explored in this chapter to illustrate how racial/cultural identity affects learning about race and culture. According to these models, VREGs and Whites vary in the extent to which members of the group identify with their racial/cultural group membership. Thus, racial/cultural identity attitudes represent the extent to which persons hold positive, negative, or mixed attitudes toward their own racial or cultural group and their place in it (i.e., their attitude regarding their racial or cultural identity). Various levels of racial/cultural identity may represent different possibilities for developing cross-cultural competence.

History and Models of Minority
Racial Identity Development

In the early 1970s, the emphasis in cross-cultural counseling training was on the need to accurately understand the client from a sociocultural context. The focus was on understanding the client's cultural roots, values (particularly if they differed from White middle-class values), perceived problems, and preferred (culturally relevant) interventions. Beginning in the early 1980s, counseling researchers began to focus on the significant within-group (or intracultural) diversity found among all racial/ethnic minority groups. Leading theories proffered to explain intracultural diversity focused on differences due to socioeconomic status, levels of acculturation (particularly in immigrant groups), and levels of racial identity commitment (particularly among African Americans).

By the mid-1980s, it had become clear that psychological research within African American communities should include an assessment of racial identity commitment (see Parham, 1989), and or other Afrocentric-bases paradigms (e.g., Baldwin & Bell, 1985; Milliones, 1980). The increasing research emphasis on racial identity (see Helms, 1990) was considered by some to be a landmark breakthrough in the still relatively young field of cross-cultural counseling.

Black Racial Identity Development Models

By far, the majority of extant racial identity research has focused on Black Americans. Helms (1990) defines Black racial identity or Nigrescence as

> The developmental process by which a person "becomes Black" where Black is defined in terms of one's manner of thinking about and evaluating oneself and one's reference groups rather than in terms of skin color per se. (Helms, 1990, p. 17)

Helms and colleagues (Cross, Parham, & Helms, 1991; Helms, 1990) provide a thorough overview of Black racial identity models and reviews the theories of Cross (1971), Jackson (1975), Milliones (1980), and Thomas (1971), among others. The most researched of these theoretical presentations, especially within the domain of counseling, is that of William Cross (1971, 1978, 1989).

Cross (1971, 1995; Hall, Cross, & Freedle, 1972) labeled his stage theory the Negro-to-Black Conversion Experience, and outlined five distinct stages during which Black people evolve from a self-view that degrades Blackness to one in which Blackness is valued and internalized in a secure and confident manner. Cross's model has been described in detail elsewhere (Helms, 1990; Parham, 1989) and is therefore only very briefly described here.

Cross's five-stage conceptualization includes the stages identified as Preencounter, Encounter, Immersion/Emersion, Internalization, and Internalization/Commitment. The Preencounter stage is characterized by an idealization of the dominant White culture, and a denigration of Black culture and values. During the Encounter stage, the individual begins to question previously held beliefs and one's role as a Black individual in a White-dominated power structure. The Encounter individual begins to validate himself or herself in terms of racial group membership. In the Immersion/Emersion stage, the Black individual begins to reject all non-

Black values, customs, and ideas, and fully immerses himself or herself into Black culture. In the Internalization stage, the Black person develops an assured, self-confident Black identity and is also comfortable in appreciating and accepting portions of non-Black worldviews. The last stage, Internalization/Commitment is similar to the previous one, but characterized by a sustained and long-term commitment to Black affairs. Cross recognized that many Blacks at the Internalization stage develop a Black identity, but do not maintain a commitment to Black issues.

One significant strength of the Cross model, in relation to other Black racial identity conceptions, is that it continues to undergo theoretical modifications and interpretations. Cross (1989, 1995) himself has continued to elaborate on the theory, while Helms has amended the model within the context of "worldviews" (Helms, 1986), and the consideration of a bimodal expression characteristic of each stage. In addition, Cross's construct has been the focus of rigorous, systematic, and experimentally varied empirical investigations, which, in the aggregate, have found a moderate to high level of content-, construct-, and predictive/discriminant-validity support for both the construct itself and the leading instrument used to operationalize the construct via the Racial Identity Attitude Scales (see reviews in Helms, 1989, 1990; Ponterotto & Wise, 1987; Sabnani & Ponterotto, 1992).

Although William Cross is credited with originally formulating the process of Black racial identity development, Janet Helms's contributions involve translating his ideas and research into a meaningful schema to view Black identity development as it relates to psychological states, mental health issues, and counseling implications. Using the classification scheme of Cross, Helms and colleagues (1990, 1995; Carter, 1995; Parham & Helms, 1981) identity development is seen as a series of five ego statuses (originally called stages) by which African Americans evolve. According to Helms, African Americans are raised and socialized in a racist society replete with negative racial stereotypes. These stereotypes and/or beliefs about themselves and others around them become internalized. The Black person comes to believe in his or her inferiority and may strive to "become White." Therefore, improving one's self-esteem and viewing the world in a realistic manner requires overcoming internalized societal racial stereotypes and the negative own-group conceptions embedded via the socialization process. Helms (1995) believes that the process of Black racial identity development means the abandonment of "internalized racism" and the development of a positive racial self-conception and group expression.

A major strength of the Helms's model is her ability to derive practical implications for understanding racial identity development. First, it is a valuable diagnostic tool for understanding the psychological frame of mind and characteristics of African American clients. Helms has been able to identify the most predominant "information processing strategies" for each ego status likely to be used by clients. In other words, each status has an associated psychological mechanism (selective perception, repression, hypervigilance, flexibility, and so on) by which the person handles racial information or situations. Second, understanding the ego statuses allows a clinician to anticipate how clients may respond and, in turn, promotes use of more relevant interventions for ameliorating race-related issues. An African American client, for example, at the Preencounter status may be favorably disposed toward seeing a White therapist whereas one at the Immersion/Emersion status might be unfavorably disposed. A counselor aware of the dynamics might choose a strategy aimed at aiding the client to see their reactions in relation to racial identity. Third, it strongly implies that the role of therapy should be aimed at aiding people to move to greater levels of racial consciousness, to free themselves from internalized racism, and to view the problems as potentially residing in societal forces (avoidance of victim blame) as well as in themselves. Last, Helms's formulations have broad meaning for clinical training and for societal relationships, which go beyond the therapeutic situation.

Asian American Identity Development Models

Models of Asian American identity development have not advanced as far as those relating to Black identity. Nevertheless, early formulations involved both type and process proposals. An early heuristic one was developed by Sue and Sue (1971) in which they proposed three different Chinese American personality types: (a) Traditionalist: A person who internalizes traditional Chinese customs and values, resists acculturation forces, and believes in the "old ways"; (b) Marginal Person: A person who attempts to assimilate and acculturate into White society, rejects traditional Chinese ways, internalizes society's negativism toward minority groups, and may develop racial-self hatred; and (c) Asian American: A person who is in the process of forming a positive identity, who is ethnically and politically aware, and who becomes increasingly bicultural. Sue and Sue (1971) used this framework to describe the types of issues likely to arise from Chinese American clients in the counseling/therapy process.

Another "type" model was subsequently proposed by Kitano (1982) to account for Japanese American role behaviors with respect to Japanese and U.S. cultures. Four types were formulated: (a) Positive-Positive, in which the person identifies with both Japanese and White cultures without role conflicts; (b) Negative-Positive in which there is a rejection of White culture and acceptance of Japanese American culture with accompanying role conflicts; (c) Positive-Negative in which the person accepts White culture and rejects Japanese culture with concomitant role conflict; and (d) Negative-Negative in which one rejects both.

Although there have been other Asian American "type" models offered (Lee, 1991), most suffer from several limitations. First, they do not seem to address how an individual develops one ethnic identity type over another. Although they were useful in describing characteristics of the type, they represented static entities rather than a dynamic process of identity development. Second, the proposal of the "types" seems too simplistic to account for the complexity of racial identity development. Third, these models tend to concentrate on only one Asian American ethnic group (Chinese American or Japanese American only) and one wonders whether they are equally applicable to Korean Americans, Filipino Americans, Vietnamese Americans, and so on. Last, other than a few empirical studies (Lee, 1991; Sue & Frank, 1973) empirical testing of these typologies is seriously lacking.

Responding to these criticisms, several investigators have begun to move toward the development of stage/process models of Asian American identity development (Atkinson, Morten, & Sue, 1993; Kim, 1981; Lee, 1991). Stage/process models tend to view identity formation as occurring in stages from less healthy to more healthy evolutions. With each stage there exists a constellation of traits and characteristics associated with racial/ethnic identity. They also attempt to explain the conditions or situations that might retard, enhance, or impel the individual forward. Because the Atkinson et al. (1993) model has become a general minority identity development model and will be discussed later, we have chosen to briefly discuss only the earlier one proposed by Kim (1981).

After a thorough review of the literature, Kim (1981) used a qualitative narrative approach with third-generation Japanese American women to posit a progressive and sequential stage model of Asian American identity development: Ethnic Awareness, White Identification, Awakening to Social Political Consciousness, Redirection to Asian American Consciousness, and Incorporation. Her model incorporates the influence of acculturation, exposure to cultural differences, environmental negativism to racial differences, personal methods of handling race-related conflicts, and the effects of group or social movements on the Asian American individual.

1. The *Ethnic Awareness* stage begins around the ages of 3-4 when the child's family members serve as the significant ethnic group model. Positive or

neutral attitudes toward one's own ethnic origin are formed depending on the amount of ethnic exposure conveyed by the caretakers.

2. The *White Identification* stage begins when children enter school where peers and the surroundings become powerful forces in conveying racial prejudice, which negatively impacts their self-esteem and identity. The realization of "differentness" from such interactions leads to self-blame and a desire to escape their own racial heritage by identifying with White society.

3. The *Awakening to Social Political Consciousness* stage means the adoption of a new perspective, often correlated with increased political awareness. Kim believes that the civil rights and women's movements and other significant political events often precipitate this new awakening. The primary result is an abandoning of identification with White society and a consequent understanding of oppression and oppressed groups.

4. The *Redirection* stage means a reconnection or renewed connection with one's Asian American heritage and culture. This is often followed by a realization of White oppression as the culprit for the negative experiences of youth. Anger against White racism may become a defining theme with concomitment increases of Asian American self and group pride.

5. The *Incorporation* stage represents the highest form of identity evolution. It encompasses the development of a positive and comfortable identity as Asian American and consequent respect for other racial/cultural heritages. Identification for or against White culture is no longer an important issue.

Latino(a)/Hispanic American Identity Development Models

Although a number of ethnic identity development models have been formulated to account for Hispanic identity (Bernal & Knight, 1993; Casas & Pytluk, 1995; Szapocznik, Santisteban, Kurtines, Hervis, & Spencer, 1982), the one most similar to those of African Americans and Asian Americans is proposed by Ruiz (1990). His model was formulated from a clinical perspective via case studies of Chicano/Latino subjects. Several underlying assumptions are made by Ruiz. First, he believed in a culture-specific explanation of identity for Chicano, Mexican American, and Latino clients. Although models about other ethnic group development or the more general ones were helpful, they lacked the specificity of Hispanic cultures. Second, the marginal status of Latinos is highly correlated with maladjustment. Third, negative experiences of forced assimilation are considered destructive to an individual. Fourth, having pride in one's cultural heritage and ethnic identity is positively correlated with mental health. Last, pride in one's ethnicity affords the Hispanic greater freedom to choose freely. These beliefs underlie the following five-stage model.

1. *Causal:* During this period messages, injunctions from the environment or significant others, or both either affirm, ignore, negate, or denigrate the ethnic heritage of the person. Affirmation of one's ethnic identity is lacking and the person may experience traumatic or humiliating experiences related to ethnicity. There is a failure to identify with Latino culture.

2. *Cognitive:* As a result of negative/distorted messages, three erroneous belief systems about Chicano/Latino heritage becomes incorporated into mental sets: (a) association of ethnic group membership with poverty and prejudice, (b) assimilation to White society is the only means of escape, and (c) assimilation is the only possible road to success.

3. *Consequence:* Fragmentation of ethnic identity becomes very noticeable and evident. The person feels ashamed, embarrassed by ethnic markers such as name, accent, skin color, cultural customs, and so on. The unwanted self-image leads to estrangement, and rejection of Chicano/Latino heritage.

4. *Working Through:* Two major dynamics distinguish this stage. First, the person becomes increasingly unable to cope with the psychological distress of ethnic identity conflict. Second, the person can no longer be a "pretender" by identifying with an alien ethnic identity. The person is propelled to reclaim and reintegrate disowned ethnic identity fragments. Ethnic consciousness increases.

5. *Successful Resolution:* This last stage is exemplified by greater acceptance of his or her culture and ethnicity. There is an improvement in self-esteem and a sense that ethnic identity represents a positive and success-promoting resource.

The Ruiz (1990) model has a subjective reality missing in many of the empirically based ones. This is expected because it was formulated through a clinical population. It has the added advantage of suggesting intervention focus and direction for each of the stages. For example, the focus of counseling in the Causal stage is the disaffirming and restructuring of the injunctions; for the Cognitive stage, it is the use of cognitive strategies attacking faulty beliefs; for the Consequence stage, it is reintegration of ethnic identity fragments in a positive manner; for the Working Through stage, ethnocultural identification issues are important; and for the Successful Resolution stage, the promotion of a positive identity becomes important.

General Minority Identity Development Models

Since the appearance of racial/cultural identity development models in the literature, the number of similar conceptions for other culturally distinct groups has exploded on the scene. Models of "Indianness" or acculturation for American Indians (Choney, Berryhill-Paapke, & Robbins, 1995; Ryan & Ryan, 1989; Zitzow & Estes, 1981), feminist identity development (Downing & Roush, 1985; McNamara & Richard, 1989), biracial identity development (Kerwin & Ponterotto, 1995; Root, 1992), and gay/lesbian identity development (McCarn & Fassinger, 1996) suggest similar processes and may attest to an experiential reality common to "minority status."

Partially in response to the strong research focus on Black racial identity, and partialy because it was believed that the construct of Black identity development could in part generalize to other oppressed groups, Atkinson et al. (1989) developed the minority identity development (MID) model. The five-stage MID model is anchored in the belief that all minority groups experience the common force of oppression, and as a result, all will generate attitudes and behaviors consistent with a natural internal struggle to develop a strong sense of self- and group-identity in spite of oppressive conditions. The MID model is presented as a stage theory, however, the authors caution that the model is best conceptualized as a continuous process in which the stages blend into one another without clear or abrupt demarcations.

Each stage in the MID model is defined with respect to four attitudinal groupings: (a) attitudes toward oneself; (b) attitudes toward others in the same reference group; (c) attitudes toward members of other minority groups; and (d) attitudes toward the White majority group. The five stages are briefly described next.

The Conformity stage is highlighted by the minority individual's preference for dominant-group cultural values and norms. The reader will note the conceptual similarities between this stage and Cross's (1995) Pre-encounter stage. In Stage 2, Dissonance, the individual experiences a breakdown of his or her previously held denial system (active during the previous stage), and begins to develop an awareness of minority-group strengths. Feelings of shame and embarrassment are common to this stage as the individual evaluates his or her previously held Conformity attitudes. This stage parallels the Encounter stage in the Cross (1995) model.

The third stage in the MID model is Resistance and Immersion. Here the minority individual comes to completely endorse the norms/values of his or her reference group, while at the same time rejecting White middle-class cultural norms. Attitudes and feelings in this stage parallel those common to Cross's (1995) Immersion/Emersion stage. During the Introspection stage, the minority person begins to question his or her rigidly held cultural views, and begins to direct increased attention to individual self-view and autonomy. Finally, in Stage 5, Synergetic Articulation and Awareness, the minority individual has come to a psychologically healthy balance with regard to attitudes toward self, toward others of the same minority group, toward different minority groups, and toward the majority group. This stage is characterized by a sense of self-fulfillment with regard to cultural identity, and an individual sense of high self-worth and self-confidence. In comparison to the Nigrescence model, this final MID stage, in conjunction with the previous stage, would be encompassed in Cross's (1995) Internalization stage.

Summary of Minority Identity Development Models

In our very brief review of the Cross (1995) and Atkinson, Mortensen and Sue (1993) models, we could not do justice to the theoretical and applied importance of these identity constructs. For a comprehensive discussion of these models, complete with counseling implications, the reader is referred to Helms (1990) and Atkinson, Mortensen and Sue (1993), respectively.

As in WRID, all models of racial/cultural identity essentially share the idea that individuals may vary from lower to higher levels of racial/cultural identity and that one level may be dominant during particular points in his or her life. Also, most models suppose that awareness at each level involves attitudes about self that, in turn, shape how one views the primary out-group. For Whites, this group is thought by some to be Blacks and others VREGs. For many VREGs, the out-group are members of the dominant group—in this case Whites. Therefore, in describing racial/cultural identity, a broad discussion of identity development is intended to include all major racial/cultural groups in the United States. Keep in mind, however, the differences in sociopolitical power among the groups. Due to the power differences, Whites, as members of the dominant racial group in the U.S., may experience a different racial identity.

At the first level, minority individuals believe that what is important is the person, not the color. Thus, they are not aware of themselves in racial terms; in other words, the Level 1 person denies that racial/cultural issues matter. They look to and emulate Euro-Americans and institutions. These individuals consider themselves to be good Americans. For VREG individuals, they become true believers of the work ethic and may want to be accepted by the dominant group. Therefore, they may downplay their race and racial heritage. Because they believe that race is unimportant, they are unable or unwilling to learn about their own race and culture. So minimal self-awareness about racial/cultural beliefs, attitudes, and values is developed. They will not be able to develop racially and culturally based knowledge nor will they develop racially and culturally adaptive counseling skills. A trainee at this level of racial/cultural identity development will probably see culture in terms of individual differences but not in terms of group differences. As a counselor, a person with a predominance of Level 1 attitudes would perhaps have difficulty learning about race or cultural topics because his or her racial/cultural identity does not include consideration of the importance of racial/cultural issues. As a consequence, the counselor would tend not to exhibit the beliefs, attitudes, knowledge, or skills required of one who is culturally competent.

At Level 2, the individual has an experience that challenges his or her previous view. The person becomes aware of social norms and pressures associated with cross-racial interactions. During Level 2, the person is forced to acknowledge that he or she is African American, Asian American, Latino(a)/Hispanic American, or Native American. The awareness of being a racial/ethnic person is presumed to be associated with increased realization of racism and one's behavior in accord with racial norms. The awareness of being a racial/ethnic person is accompanied by feelings of guilt, depression, and confusion. The individual begins to view his or her racial identity more positively and works to become deeply involved in learning and experiencing the meaning and values of his or her race and unique culture. Race is beginning to be seen as an important issue, but the individual at this level of racial awareness is still not clear about how race is important to him or her. A counselor at this level of racial identity might be able to attain some knowledge and to that extent and degree may be able to begin to explore his or her own beliefs and attitudes;, he or she would possess only a low level of cultural competence. She or he would still not have much self-awareness about racial/cultural beliefs, attitudes, and values—nor would they have developed racially and culturally based knowledge, or any useful racially and culturally adaptive counseling skills. Such a trainee or counselor might feel overwhelmed and confused in cross-cultural training. The desire to learn, however, may move them on to the next level.

During Level 3, the individual becomes immersed in his or her race and culture. One's own group becomes idealized and others are judged based on the standards and values of one's own race and culture. Level 3 attitudes seem to be characterized by an awareness of race and culture in a way that is constrained from developing cultural competence because of the extreme hostility and anger characteristic of this level. The counselor or trainee is aware of his or her own racial/cultural heritage but is not yet able to value and respect cultural differences; the person is not aware of his or her own biases with respect to racial/cultural groups. Consequently, he or she is not comfortable with differences due to race and cultural beliefs.

The racial/cultural information the counselor holds at this level is often distorted by selective perception. Thus a trainee or counselor would be limited in his or her ability to work with clients from different groups when race, culture, or both were counseling issues. Continued interest and work in cross-racial issues eventually lead to more accurate information and beliefs.

When the trainee or counselor enters Level 4, the individual typically is secure in and proud of his or her racial/cultural identity. Level 4 attitudes seem to be characterized by a broad and flexible understanding of race/culture and, as such, an individual at this level is able to develop cross-cultural competence. A person has evolved to a level of racial identity such that he or she is aware of his or her own racial-/cultural-based values, is aware of racial stereotypes and works to confront the tendency to label or hold preconceived notions about race or culture, and recognizes racial/cultural differences and does not profess to be colorblind.

Level 5 development suggests that the person would also use her or his knowledge and skills in socially active ways.

In summary, the process associated with developing cross-cultural competence involves developing racial/cultural identity. This may occur by way of the training environment or through individual self-exploration. However it occurs, it seems that it is essential for one to presume to be competent across races and cultures. It appears that through the identity process one may begin to value him or herself as a racial/cultural being and, as a consequence, learn to value and understand members of other racial/cultural groups. Only in this way is one able to develop cross-cultural competence. The work on these models has led us to focus more attention to the knowledge and skills related to racial identity development and to introduce two new competencies to the original Sue et al. (1992) report.

To the original *Journal of Counseling and Development* Sue et al. (1992) article, in the section Developing Appropriate Intervention Strategies and Techniques, subhead Knowledge, Number 6, and subhead Skills, Number 8, respectively, we add the following:

6. The culturally skilled psychologist or counselor has knowledge of models of minority and majority identity models, and understands how these models relate to the counseling relationship and the counseling process.

and

8. The culturally skilled psychologist or counselor can tailor his or her relationship-building strategies, intervention plans, and referral considerations to the particular stage of identity development of the client, while taking into account his or her own level of racial identity development.

It is clear that the study of minority identity development models is central to cross-cultural counseling training. In Chapter 5, we emphasized the importance of understanding the racial identity of Whites as well. The multicultural counseling interaction is a complex and involved process (Pedersen, 1988), and it is a two-way interactive one. Ponterotto (1988) has emphasized the need to examine the counselor's level of racial identity when researching the counseling process. This means devoting extensive research efforts to White racial identity development given that the overwhelming majority of counselors and psychologists are White.

Conclusion

In the over 16 years since the publication of the first competency report, a number of new research directions for the field have emerged. A leading new theoretical and research direction termed *racial identity development* focuses on understanding how both clients and counselors come to accept themselves as racial beings in a racist society. It is now believed that racial identity development is a central component of counseling training, for all trainees, regardless of race or geographic locale. It is hoped that this brief overview of minority and majority racial identity development will stimulate increased research in the area.

7

Multicultural Counseling Competencies

Developing Culturally Appropriate Intervention Strategies

MULTICULTURAL COUNSELING COMPETENCE IS . . .

- Freeing ourselves from traditional definitions of counseling and psychotherapy:
    Focus on the individual
    Verbal and emotional expressiveness
    Self-disclosure
    Insight
- Expanding the boundaries of professional practice and the repertoire of our interpersonal helping skills (a much more action oriented and directive style).
- Expanding and using alternative helping roles:
    Adviser
    Advocate
    Consultant
    Change agent
    Facilitator of indigenous support systems
    Facilitator of indigenous healing systems
- Learning from indigenous models of healing:
    Holistic outlook on life
    Importance of spirituality in being
    Existence and use of different planes of reality

A culturally skilled counselor is one who is in the process of actively developing and practicing appropriate, relevant, and sensitive intervention strategies and skills in working with his or her culturally different clients. . . . It is recognized that extrapsychic as well as intrapsychic approaches may be more appropriate and that differential helping strategies may be needed. (Sue, Arredondo, & McDavis, 1991, p. 481)

MCT theory stresses the importance of multiple helping roles developed by many culturally different groups and societies. Besides the basic one-on-one encounter aimed at remediation in the individual, these roles often involve larger social units, systems intervention, and prevention. That is, the conventional roles of counseling and psychotherapy are only one of many others available to the helping professional. (Sue, Ivey, & Pedersen, 1996, pp. 20-21)

Culturally competent helping is related to several factors. First, counselors must be able to free themselves from the confining Euro-American definitions of counseling. As we have seen, conventional counseling or therapy roles dictate what is considered to be therapeutic behavior within the sessions. Both these roles and behaviors are culture bound and potentially unhelpful or oppressive to culturally different clients. Second, clinicians must begin to expand the range of their helping behaviors. Most mental health professionals are products of graduate training programs that are governed by standards of practice and codes of ethics that prescribe a very narrow band of behavior considered to be appropriate. Third, culturally relevant counseling and therapy demand a broader range of helping roles played by the therapist. The one-to-one therapy session conducted in a sterile office, far removed from the real world, and aimed primarily at remediation may be ineffective when the source of problems resides in the environment. Fourth, familiarity and the ability to incorporate non-Western indigenous forms of healing contributes much to the multiculturally competent helping professional. Last, there is a need for psychologists to understand and be able to intervene on a larger systemic basis by creating multicultural organizations (discussed in Chapters 8 and 9).

Freeing Ourselves From Traditional Definitions of Counseling and Psychotherapy

In Euro-American society, being a professional psychologist, counselor, or therapist is influenced by the values, knowledge base, and beliefs of our society. Because the theories of counseling and psychotherapy originate from a particular cultural context, it can be said that they also reflect those biases in definitions of normality-abnormality, human development, and both the goals and processes of therapy (Sue et al., 1996). As a result, the standards for providers of services are necessarily infused with primarily Eurocentric cultural values and assumptions (Parham, 1997). They may be applicable to one cultural group, but when applied to another, may constitute cultural oppression. Let us briefly try to define and unmask the cultural assumptions inherent in most forms of counseling and psychotherapy.

Counseling and therapy can be defined as the systematic application of techniques, derived from predominantly Eurocentric psychological principles, by trained (licensed or certified) mental health professionals, and for the purpose of helping psychologically troubled people. Depending on theoretical orientation (psychodynamic, behavioral, cognitive, and so on) and perspective, counselors may attempt to modify attitudes, thoughts, feelings, or behaviors; to help clients attain insight and rational control; to enhance self-actualization and mental health; to make clients feel better; to change a self-concept; to remove the cause of a psychological problem; or to encourage adaptation (Sue, Sue, & Sue, 1997). Although mental health professionals often pride themselves on the scientific basis of their practice, it is more often "art" than science. This aspect of clinical practice makes it especially prone to reflect the cultural assumptions of the wider society. And, despite the fact that theories of counseling attempt to emphasize how they differ from one another, most seem to share some common therapeutic features (Sue, 1997). Four of these appear particularly problematic when inappropriately applied.

1. Most forms of counseling and psychotherapy focus on the individual. As a result, uniqueness, autonomy, and independence are highly valued and may be used as markers of maturity, healthy functioning, and mental health. Groups that stress a much more collectivistic identity in which the psycho-social unit of operation is the family, group, or collective society may have their members inappropriately labeled as "immature," "overly dependent," and "unable to make decisions on their own."

2. Verbal and emotional expressiveness is an underlying therapeutic process and outcome of counseling. We value people in therapy who are verbal, articulate, and able to express their thoughts and feelings. Unfortunately, therapists often fail to realize that differences in styles of communication and the heavier reliance on nonverbal communication by certain cultural groups may make them prone to being labeled "inhibited," "out of touch with their feelings," "repressed," and exhibiting a "poverty of thought."

3. Self-disclosure and discussion of the most intimate aspects of one's hopes, fears, and aspirations are hallmarks of counseling. For racial/ethnic minority groups, both cultural and sociopolitical forces may prevent such behaviors in

the counseling process. Among traditional Asians and Asian Americans, for example, intimate matters are only revealed to close acquaintances and not strangers (therapists). Likewise, because many minorities experience prejudice and discrimination, they may harbor a healthy distrust of White counselors. As a result, they may be reluctant to self-disclose. An unenlightened therapist may see such clients as "guarded," "suspicious," or "paranoid."

4. Most mental health professionals place great value on insight—the ability to understand the basis of one's motivations, perceptions, and behaviors. Many cultures may not value or perceive that insight is the road to mental health. Among certain Asian groups, for example, "avoidance of morbid thinking" and not insight is the desired goal. Likewise, insight may be class bound, in that it assumes clients have time to engage in self-exploration for the future. When feeding one's family, obtaining proper medical care, or finding a job are the immediate and pressing needs for those in poverty, insight may seem totally inappropriate. Thus, culturally different clients are often perceived as "lacking in insight" or "not psychologically minded" when in reality they are concerned with "survival."

In addition to these attributes, counseling and psychotherapy practice may be said to value competitiveness rather than cooperation, linear-static time emphasis, nuclear versus extended family, internal locus of responsibility, and an empirical approach to asking and answering questions about the human condition (Sue, 1994). These characteristics of mental health practice are not necessarily right or wrong, good or bad. The main point is that they reflect a Euro-American worldview, which, when applied to culturally different groups, may become culturally oppressive. The culturally competent and skilled counselor must not only be in touch with his or her own worldviews and values, but must also be able to deconstruct the cultural and class values inherent in practice. This awareness allows the culturally skilled helping professional to (a) free himself or herself from the cultural conditioning of his or her training, (b) compare and contrast the appropriateness of both the process and goals of counseling, and (c) begin developing culturally appropriate techniques and strategies.

Encapsulation of Professional Practice: Expanding the Boundaries

Therapeutic practice is directly governed by the code of ethics and standards of practice of our professional associations. In the past, both the American Counseling Association and the American Psychological Association did little to directly address issues of diversity or to consider the cultural encapsulation of these standards. Increasingly, however, both professional organizations and those associated with other mental health disciplines have become sensitized to these charges. The revised ACA *Code of Ethics and Standards of Practice* (American Counseling Association, 1995) has taken positive steps to rectify these serious inadequacies. In the Preamble, the following statement is found: "The American Counseling Association is an educational, scientific, and professional organization whose members are dedicated to the enhancement of human development throughout the life-span. Association members *recognize diversity in our society and embrace a cross-cultural approach* in support of the worth, dignity, potential, and uniqueness of each individual" (italics added). Statements regarding nondiscrimination are included throughout: "Counselors do not condone or engage in discrimination based on age, color, culture, disability, ethnic group, gender, race, religion, sexual orientation, marital status, or socioeconomic status."

Likewise, APA's *Ethical Principles of Psychologists and Code of Conduct* (American Psychological Association, 1992), and the *Accreditation Handbook* (American Psychological Association, 1986), contain similar statements: "Psychologists do not engage in unfair discrimination based on age, gender, race, ethnicity, national origin, religion, sexual orientation, disability, socioeconomic status, or any basis proscribed by law. . . . Psychologists attempt to identify situations in which particular interventions . . . may not be applicable or may require adjustment in administration . . . such as individuals' gender, age, race, ethnicity, national origin, religion, sexual orientation, disability, language, or socioeconomic status."

It remains to be seen, however, whether these admirable statements represent hollow words or an actual commitment to the concepts of multiculturalism and diversity. That they are not operationalized or translated into more meaningful suggestions is disturbing. Thus, the mental health profession may continue to operate from certain narrowly prescribed "therapeutic behaviors" and roles. For example, most mental health professionals continue to be taught that therapists (a) do not give advice and suggestions because it may foster dependency, (b) do not self-disclose their thoughts and feelings because a therapist should be objective and not let personal values enter the session, (c) do not take a teaching role, (d) do not accept gifts from their clients because it unduly obligates them resulting in lost objectivity, and (e) do not enter into dual or multiple relationships because establishing boundaries are important and because of the potential conflicts of interest. Thus, clinical practice is defined as working for the therapeutic good of the individual client, avoiding undue influence, allowing clients to make decisions on their own, setting clear boundaries, and maintaining objectivity.

Parham (1997) notes that these therapeutic taboos are infused with Eurocentric assumptions and values. When speaking of African Americans, he emphasizes African-centered ethical codes that are grounded in human relations and the interconnectedness between the helper and the helpee. Developing and maintaining emotional and spiritual connectedness is considered facilitative. Parham states, "application of an African-centered worldview will cause one to question the need for objectivity absent emotions, the need for distance rather than connectedness, and the need for dichotomous relationships rather than multiple roles." Sue et al. (1996) suggest that multiculturally effective counseling and therapy involve broadening the perspective and repertoire of helping.

Ivey's work (Ivey, 1981, 1986; Nwachuku & Ivey, 1991) presents clear evidence that different theoretical orientations dictate different skill patterns in the helping behavior of professionals. For example, many of the major theories tend to advocate more nondirect and passive attending and helping skills in the counseling session. Counselors and therapists, for example, are likely to use predominantly attending skills (minimal encouragers, questioning, reflection of feelings, paraphrasing, summarizing, and so on) while avoiding the more active skills (giving advice and suggestions, disclosing therapist thoughts and feelings, taking a teaching role, and so on). These latter attributes are considered to be therapeutically less sound, prone to therapist bias, takes away the decision-making responsibility from clients or may unduly influence them. These therapeutic guidelines are strongly based on Euro-American cultural values and beliefs, but fail to consider potential cultural and sociopolitical factors.

Different cultural groups have different definitions or beliefs about what constitutes a helping relationship. Among Asian and many Asian American groups, for example, a helping relationship is characterized by the following attributes: (a) subtlety and indirectness in communications, (b) vertical or hierarchical communication patterns, (c) respect for authority figures, and (d) the giving of advice and directions by a perceived expert. Note that these characteristics may clash with those of Euro-American-based therapies described earlier. In counseling and therapy, the client is expected to be the more active of the participants, the giving of advice and directions is a traditional taboo, interpretation and confrontation is often used, and the relationship between therapist and client is more egalitarian. Sue et al. (1996) state "For many Asian American clients, the helpful counselor may be one who gives advice and suggestions, avoids confrontation and direct interpretation of motives and actions, indirectly discusses personal issues, does more initial talking than the client, and evidences a formal interactive approach." Traditional Asian American clients may attribute low credibility and expertise to a Euro-American-trained counselor or therapist (Atkinson, Morten, & Sue, 1993). These counseling responses or approach may be lacking in the behavioral repertoire of counselors because they have not been trained to see helping in such a manner. Thus, even if they see the necessity of such an approach, they may feel uncomfortable in altering their characteristic style of helping.

Likewise, it is becoming clear that counseling and psychotherapy are also embedded in the wider sociopolitical forces of our society. Issues of race relations and the power differentials existing between different groups in our society are often played out in the counseling relationship. Because the history of the United States is very much tied to the oppressive treatment of racial/ethic minorities, many culturally different clients may enter the therapeutic relationship with great suspicion and wariness. They are likely to approach the helping professional with the following questions and thoughts: "What makes you any different from other White folks who have oppressed me?" "What makes you immune from inheriting the racial biases of your forebears?" "Why should I trust you?" "How open and honest are you about your biases?" "Before I open up to you, I need to know where you're coming from."

Racial/ethnic minorities and other oppressed groups are not likely to unconditionally trust a White counselor. They are likely to test the helping professional, to ascertain the answers to these questions, and to make a decision regarding the trustworthiness of the helper. The testing may be quite overt and direct such as confronting the counselor with the question "Are you a racist?" to more subtle statements such as "Most people could care less about minorities." How the professional deals with these challenges will either enhance or diminish the trustworthiness of the counselor. A therapist who fails to directly address the first question or chooses not to express a personal thought about the latter statement may seriously impair his or her credibility. In addition, a failure to adequately deal with these tests means the culturally different client will not self-disclose their most intimate thoughts and feelings. To adequately deal with such a situation requires two things that conventional counseling and therapy limits: counselor self-disclosure and an active approach. Interestingly, studies continue to show that certain groups of Asian Americans, African Americans, American Indians, and Hispanic Americans prefer more active therapeutic approaches than nonactive ones (Atkinson & Lowe, 1995; Atkinson, Maruyama, & Matsui, 1978; Dauphinais, Dauphinais, & Rowe,

1981; Nwachuku & Ivey, 1991; Ruiz & Ruiz, 1983). Likewise, approaches that use a more nondirective and egalitarian relationship may be experienced negatively by minorities and lead to premature termination (Sue, 1995a).

Cultural flexibility in helping, expanding the repertoire of helping responses, and reconceptualizing the helping relationship in culturally relevant terms may truly enhance expertness, attractiveness and trustworthiness. Alexander and Sussman (1997) have suggested the use of music, dance, food, art, folktales, and so on as valuable creative multicultural counseling approaches. Music, for example, can be used as a means to promote racial identity development, to make minority students feel comfortable on predominantly White campuses, and to relieve anxiety over racial issues. With respect to folktales, Alexander and Sussman (1997) state: "The use of folktales is another creative way to infuse multiculturalism into the counseling relationship. Folktales reflect the client's culture and can be helpful in providing counselors with a glimpse of the types of problems faced by their client as well as problem-solving skills available to him or her. . . . Culturally relevant storytelling may facilitate a therapeutic alliance between a culturally dissimilar client and counselor because it provides the counselor with the opportunity to start where the client is and not vice versa." It is clear, then, that effective multicultural counseling and therapy dictate methods and goals consistent with the life experiences and cultural values of the client. No single theory or approach in helping are equally applicable across all situations, problems, and populations. Counselors need to be able to shift their styles to meet the cultural and sociopolitical dimensions of their diverse clientele.

Alternative Helping Roles

Because counselors are increasingly being asked to work with culturally different clients, and because they now realize that the conventional one-to-one, in-the-office, talk-form of treatment aimed at remediation of existing problems may be at odds with the sociopolitical and cultural dimensions of their clients, they are finding their traditional therapeutic roles ineffective. Calls for training programs to train mental health professionals to play alternative helping roles have increased (Atkinson, Thompson, & Grant, 1993; Pedersen, 1994; Sue et al., 1996). Three key forces are behind this movement. First, as we have seen, is that culturally different groups may not perceive or respond well to the conventional counseling or therapy roles. Second, is the increased recognition that the locus of the problem may reside outside (external/extrapsychic) rather than inside (internal/intrapsychic) the client. For example, prejudice and discrimination like racism, sexism, and homophobia may impede the healthy functioning of individuals and groups in our society. Third, to be discussed in the next section, is the impact of non-Western or indigenous forms of healing.

Alternative roles to the conventional counseling and therapy ones share certain commonalities (Sue et al., 1996): (a) They are generally characterized by the more active helping style of the helper; (b) They often involve the helper working outside the office—in the home, institution, or community of the client; (c) The role of the helper is more externally focused and directed toward changing environmental conditions such as policies and practices of an organization, enhancing job opportunities, and so on as opposed to focusing on and changing the client; (d) Clients are not perceived as having a problem (internal pathology), but as experiencing one (problematic situations); (e) The alternative roles are more prevention oriented as opposed to being primarily remediation in nature; and (f) The helper shoulders an increased responsibility for determining the course and outcome of the helping process. Some of these alternative roles have been conceptually described by Atkinson et al. (1993). Note that they do not deny the importance of the conventional counseling and therapy roles, but rather see the following as complementary ones.

1. *Adviser:* The main tasks of an adviser involve helping clients to solve or prevent potential problems, educating them about available options, and sharing with them what they may have found effective in dealing with the problematic situation. Immigrants, for example, may have minimal experience in U.S. society and might benefit immensely from advice and suggestions.

2. *Advocate:* The role entails representing the individual's or group's best interests to other individuals, groups, or institutions. Counselors may, for example, represent a person who does not speak English well and argue on their behalf for fair and equitable treatment. The role is not a neutral one and can entail political dimensions.

3. *Consultant:* This is a professional but collegial relationship in which both the helper and consultee work to impact or change a third party. Understanding of organizational dynamics and processes are a necessity for this role.

4. *Change agent:* The helper takes an action-oriented approach to changing aspects of the client's environment. In many respects this is similar to the consultant role, but the helper goes further in assuming responsibility for making changes that may be oppressing clients or groups.

5. *Facilitator of indigenous support systems:* Helpers in this role realize that culturally different clients may respond better to indigenous support systems

(the church, extended family, community elders, and so forth) in resolving their problems. They refer out or place people in contact with the cultural resources available in the community.

6. *Facilitator of indigenous healing systems:* Such a helper may take two courses of action: (a) refer clients to traditional healers such as a *curran-dismo*—Mexican folk healer—or Tai Chi Ch'uan instructor or (b) actually treat the client via indigenous healing methods. This latter action, however, assumes the counselor is skilled and knowledgeable in those healing arts.

The selection of a particular helping role, according to Atkinson et al. (1993), is dependent on several major variables. First, the helper must determine the locus of the problem. Does it reside internal to the client (weak ego control) or is it situated in the environment (biased policies and practices). Second, the level of acculturation of the client has to be ascertained. Third, are the goals primarily remediation or prevention. Space does not permit a detailed description of the excellent conceptual framework used by these authors to determine which role should be taken. The interested reader is encouraged to study the original source.

Learning From Indigenous Models of Healing

Ever since the beginning of human existence, all societies and cultural groups have developed not only their own explanations of abnormal behaviors, but their culture-specific ways of dealing with human problems and distress (Das, 1987; Harner, 1990; Lee & Armstrong, 1995). Within the United States, counseling and psychotherapy are the dominant psycho-logical healing methods; in other cultures, however, indigenous healing approaches continue to be widely used. Although there are similarities between Euro-American helping systems and the indigenous practices of many cultural groups, there are major dissimilarities as well. Western forms of counseling, for example, rely on sensory information defined by the physical plane of reality (Western science), while most indigenous methods rely on the spiritual plane of existence in seeking a cure. In keeping with the cultural encapsulation of our profession, Western healing has failed to acknowledge or learn from these age-old forms of wisdom (Highlen, 1996). Yet, in its attempt to become culturally responsive, the field of counseling must begin to put aside the biases of Western science, to acknowledge the existence of intrinsic help-giving networks, and to incorporate the legacy of ancient wisdom, which may be contained in indigenous models of healing.

The work and writings of Lee (Lee, 1995; Lee & Armstrong, 1995; Lee, Oh, & Mountcastle, 1992) are especially helpful in this regard. He has studied what is called the *universal shamanic tradition*, which encompasses the centuries-old recognition of healers within a community. The anthropological term *shaman* refers to people often called witch, witch doctor, wizard, medicine man or woman, sorcerer, or magic man or woman. These individuals are believed to possess the power to enter an altered state of consciousness and in their healing rituals journey to other planes of existence beyond the physical world. In a study of indigenous healing in 16 non-Western countries, it was found that three approaches were often used (Lee et al., 1992). First, there is heavy reliance on the use of communal, group, and family networks to shelter the disturbed individual (Saudi Arabia), to problem solve in a group context (Nigeria), and to reconnect the individual with family or significant others (Korea). Second, spiritual and religious beliefs and traditions of the community are used in the healing process. The reading of verses from the Koran and/or use of religious houses/churches are examples. Third, use of shamans (called *piris* and *fakirs* in Pakistan and Sudan) who are perceived to be the keepers of timeless wisdom is the norm. Within these approaches are embedded some valuable lessons for multicultural counseling and therapy.

1. Holistic outlook on life. Most non-Western indigenous forms of healing take a holistic outlook on well-being in that they make minimal distinction between physical and mental functioning. The interrelatedness of life forms, the environment, and the cosmos is a given. Illness, distress, or problematic behavior are seen as an imbalance of internal or external forces. The seeking of harmony or balance is the healer's goal. Among American Indians, for example, harmony with nature is symbolized by the circle, or hoop of life (Heinrich, Corbin, & Thomas, 1990). Mind, body, spirit, and nature are seen as a single unified entity with little separation between the realities of life, medicine, and religion. All forms of nature, not just the living, are to be revered because they reflect the creator or deity. Illness is seen as a break in the hoop of life, an imbalance or separation between the elements. Likewise, the Afrocentric perspective with its roots in Egypt and Nubia teaches that human beings are part of a holistic fabric and should be oriented toward collective rather than individual survival (Asante, 1987; White & Parham, 1990). The indigenous Japanese assumptions and practices of Naikan and Morita therapy attempt to move clients toward being more in tune with others and society, to move away from individualism, and to move toward interdependence and connectedness (harmony with others).

2. The importance of spirituality in being. The United States has had a long tradition in believing that one's religious beliefs should not enter into scientific or rational decisions. Incorporating religion in the conduct of therapy has generally been seen as unscientific and unprofessional. The schism occurred between religion and science centuries ago resulting in a split between science/psychology and religion (Highlen, 1994; 1996). This is often reflected in the phrase "separation of church and state." The separation has become a serious barrier to mainstream psychology incorporating indigenous forms of healing into mental health practice, especially when religion is confused with spirituality. Although people may not have a formal religion, indigenous helpers believe that spirituality is an intimate aspect of the human condition. Whereas Western psychology acknowledges the behavioral, cognitive, and affective realms, it only makes passing reference to the spiritual realm of existence. Yet, indigenous helpers believe that spirituality transcends time and space, transcends mind and body, and transcends our behaviors, thoughts, and feelings (Lee & Armstrong, 1995).

Many cultural groups place strong emphasis on the interplay and interdependence of spiritual life and healthy functioning. Puerto Ricans, for example, may sacrifice material satisfaction in favor of values pertaining to the spirit and soul. The Lakota Sioux often say *Mitakuye Oyasin* at the end of a prayer or as a salutation. Translated it means "to all my relations," which acknowledges the spiritual bond between speaker and all people present, to forebears, the tribe, the family of man, and to mother nature. It speaks to the philosophy that all life forces, mother earth, and the cosmos are sacred beings and the spiritual is the thread that binds all together. Likewise, a strong spiritual orientation has always been a major aspect of life in Africa, and during the slavery era (Hines & Boyd-Franklin, 1996). The African American churches continue to play a strong role in the lives of Black people. Increasingly, mental health professionals are becoming open to the potential benefits of spirituality as a means for coping with hopelessness, identity issues, and feelings of powerlessness. As an example of this movement, the Association for Counselor Education and Supervision recently adopted a set of competencies related to spirituality. They define spirituality as

> the animating force in life, represented by such images as breath, wind, vigor, and courage. Spirituality is the infusion and drawing out of spirit in one's life. It is experienced as an active and passive process.
>
> Spirituality is also described as a capacity and tendency that is innate and unique to all persons. This spiritual tendency moves the individual toward

knowledge, love, meaning, hope, transcendence, connectedness, and com-
passion. Spirituality includes one's capacity for creativity, growth, and the
development of a values system. Spirituality encompasses the religions,
spiritual, and transpersonal. ("Summit on Spirituality," 1997, p. 14)

3. Journeys to different planes of reality. Intrinsic to the universal
shamanic tradition is the belief in the existence of different levels or planes
of consciousness or experience. Understanding and ameliorating the causes
of illness or problems of life are often found in a different plane of reality
rather than the physical world of existence. These nonordinary reality
states are the domain of the spirit world and it is believed the human
destiny is often decided here. Shamans or indigenous helpers often enter
these realities on behalf of their clients to seek answers, to enlist the help
of the spirit world, or to aid in realigning the spiritual energy field that
surrounds the body and extends throughout the universe. Ancient Chinese
methods of healing and the Hindu chakra work acknowledges another
world of etheric reality that parallels the physical one (Highlen, 1996).
Accessing this world allows the healer to use these special energy centers
to balance and heal the body and mind. Occasionally, the shaman may aid
the helpee or novice in accessing that plane of reality, so that he or she may
find the solutions. The vision quest in conjunction with the sweat lodge
experience was used by American Indians as religious renewal or a rite of
passage (Hammerschlag, 1988; Heinrich et al., 1990). Behind these uses,
however, is the human journey to another world of reality. The ceremony
of the vision quest is intended to prepare the young man for the proper
frame of mind: use of rituals and sacred symbols, prayers to the Great
Spirit, isolation, fasting, and personal reflection. Whether in a dream state
or in full consciousness, another world of reality is said to reveal itself.
Hindu mantras, chants, meditation, and the taking of certain drugs (peyote)
all have as their purpose to allow a journey into another world of existence.
    In general, indigenous healing methods have much to offer to Euro-
American forms of mental health practice. The contributions are not only
valuable because of the multiple belief systems that now exist in our
society, but counseling and psychotherapy have neglected to deal with the
spiritual dimension of human existence. Our heavy reliance on "science"
and the reductionistic approach to treating clients have made us view
human beings and human behavior as composed of separate noninteracting
parts (cognitive, behavioral, and affective). There has been a failure to
recognize our spiritual being and to take a holistic outlook on life. Indigenous models of healing remind us of these shortcomings and challenge us
to look for answers in other realms of existence besides the physical world.

8

Multicultural Organizational Development

Lessons From the Community Mental Health Movement

MULTICULTURAL COUNSELING COMPETENCE IS . . .

- Being knowledgeable about the lessons learned from the community mental health movement.
- Understanding that institutions (policies, practices, programs, and structures) are often monocultural in nature and serve as impediments to multiculturalism.
- Learning from workforce diversity models as they apply to organizations.
- Being able to identity the characteristics of developing from a monocultural to a multicultural organization:
    Cultural destructiveness
    Cultural incapacity
    Cultural blindness
    Cultural precompetence
    Cultural competence

Researchers in organizational development and psychology have pointed out the need for U.S. businesses and other institutions to acknowledge and use the skills and talents of an increasingly multicultural workforce. They argue that competitive business practices and changing demographics should provide ample motivation for organizations to fundamentally restructure their internal cultures to accommodate diversity, and that the concept of "managing diversity" will become a dominant paradigm in management science (Copeland, 1988; Sue, 1991b, 1995b; Thomas, 1990), replacing a model based on White, male cultural norms.

It seems both logical and imperative, then, that community mental health organizations, counseling and clinical training programs, and our professional organizations adopt the insights from multiculturalism and its relationship to organizational development. Although there is evidence that community mental health services have historically embraced the goals of multiculturalism, there is less evidence that they have been able to make use of the research and implement strategies for becoming a culturally responsive system of care.

The goals of the following two chapters are (a) to review the social, political, and historical factors that have shaped the systemic development of multicultural awareness in the counseling/mental health professions, (b) to describe the conceptual framework needed for organizational multicultural competencies, and (c) to suggest ways of implementing multicultural policies and practices within the general mental health system.

Recent History of the Community Mental Health System

The community mental health movement in the United States is nearly four decades old, and has encompassed major changes in the policies, institutions, and service delivery procedures that characterized mental health services prior to the late 1950s and early 1960s. Responding to the nightmare conditions in large state mental hospitals, professional criticisms of traditional mental health treatments, advances in drug therapies, and the sociopolitical idealism that characterized the Kennedy and early Johnson administrations, Congress passed the landmark Mental Health Centers Act of 1963. The Act called for the closing of large institutions and basing the treatment of the mentally ill in their home communities, where community mental health centers (CMHCs) would provide a continuum of services (Isaac & Armat, 1990).

The federal government was to provide guidance and funding for innovative models of treatment, while each state was to develop its own agency for assessing and meeting the needs of its communities, including those unserved and underserved populations. The goal was to create a network of 2,000 centers across the nation, each serving a "catchment area" of approximately 75,000 to 200,000 people (Vega & Murphy, 1990).

This ambitious and idealistic movement coincided with the broader civil rights movement, and offered many opportunities for people to address the mental health needs of minority communities—specifically, African American, Hispanic/Latino American, Asian American, and American Indian populations. These communities were, and are, perceived to share certain histories of discrimination and oppression, based on skin color and non-European origins. Many mental health advocates argued that all minority groups needed to form coalitions, to avoid being pitted against each other during the process of community organizing, and to emphasize their shared experiences with the inadequacies of the White-dominated mental health system (Alvarez et al., 1976; Gallegos, 1982).

Critics of the mental health system pointed to many issues related to the need for culturally sensitive programs: the increasing percentages of "minority group" members in the U.S. population, and the serious underrepresentation of minorities as consumers of mental health services (Ridley, 1985; Sue & Sue, 1990). Other critics began to point at the lack of attention that predominantly White mental health professionals paid to minority clients, who were often prejudged as likely to be professionally and financially less rewarding than middle-class White patients (Gallegos, 1982).

Psychological and counseling practices were criticized as reflecting a White, Eurocentric, male, and usually middle-class point of view, and thereby defining all those people not meeting these norms as deviant or pathological. More specifically, psychological research and practices concerning ethnic and linguistic minorities frequently were based on models that described differences as deficiencies: first, that minorities were inherently inferior based on genetics or biology, also known as the "scientific racism model," and second, the "cultural deficit model," which rejected biological explanations for minority "inferiority," but concluded that minorities were likely to come from culturally "impoverished" environments that lacked the intellectual, artistic, and moral benefits of White, middle-class culture (Carter, 1995; Sue & Sue, 1990).

Minority group members were significantly underrepresented within the counseling professions and in training programs, where the few minority students enrolled often received inadequate support and validation for their cultural knowledge and identities (Atkinson, Morten, & Sue, 1993, 1998). Finally, racism was identified by critics not only as causing mental health problems for minorities, but as a pathology among Whites that called for treatment by mental health professionals as part of the goals of new community-based programs (Alvarez et al., 1976).

Many critics also argued that if counselors could take the lead in addressing social conflicts, not just intrapersonal ones, they could thereby have a positive impact on the environmental factors affecting community mental health (Isaac & Armat, 1990). Mental health reformers advocated adopting a public health/primary prevention model for addressing community needs. Poverty, poor housing, and political underrepresentation were all identified as issues contributing to the poor mental health of minority communities, and by extension, needed to be addressed in the provision of mental health services (Alvarez et al., 1976).

Despite a general acknowledgment by policymakers of many of the issues described previously, the Community Mental Health Centers Act did not explicitly address the issue of services for minorities. Although some of the early programs were designed to meet the needs of minority communities, few did so, and even fewer did so with any success (Alvarez et al., 1976; Isaac & Armat, 1990). Even though the Civil Rights Act of 1964 applied to all mental health agencies receiving federal funding (the vast majority), it was not until 1975 that amendments were actually added to the CMHC Act that specifically pertained to cultural minorities. CMHCs "serving a population including a substantial proportion of individuals of limited English-speaking ability" were explicitly required to have developed a plan and made arrangements responsive to the needs of such population for providing services to the extent practicable in the language and cultural context most appropriate to such individuals, and identified an individual on its staff who is fluent in both that language and English and whose responsibilities shall include providing guidance to such individuals and to appropriate staff members with respect to cultural sensitivities and bridging linguistic and cultural differences. (Sec. 206 (c), Public Law 94-63, 1975, as cited in Vega & Murphy, 1990, p. 7)

It was not only the lack of legislative directives that kept community mental health services from addressing the needs of minority communities. Vega and Murphy (1990) argue that despite the awareness of issues pertaining to the needs of minority communities, the community mental health movement never developed the theoretical concepts that would allow connection of these needs to systematic institutional reform. Mental health workers set themselves to change the social environment and to transcend their traditional roles by trying out community and local political organizing. They did so without much of a theoretical blueprint, much less the opportunity to systematically test experimental ideas. The result was "role confusion, professional rivalries, and organizational conflicts. Mental health professionals, who had never received the training appropriate for their new obligations, were now being asked to set up shop in unfamiliar social and cultural settings, and to develop a delivery system from an array of disparate services" (Vega & Murphy, 1990, p. 7). These same well-intentioned professionals, mostly White, were also sometimes perceived as being agents of the repressive system they hoped to reform, and were rejected by minority communities (Alvarez et al., 1976; Isaac & Armat, 1990).

One of the widely accepted ideas for addressing these concerns and for involving minority community members in the provision of mental health services was the notion of using "paraprofessionals." Community members, many of whom had been informal providers of counseling and support, would receive training that, in the best cases, might culminate in an AA degree, and allow them to function as "associate mental health workers" or "associate case workers." In practice, these positions often became dead-end jobs that offered virtually no decision- or policy-making power within systems that clung to conventional "professional" power structures (Alvarez et al., 1976). Meanwhile, the relatively few minority mental health professionals available had been trained in traditional, White-dominated programs, and therefore had only marginally more or different resources to bring to the process of designing "minority" mental health services.

Many fundamental problems besides ethnocentrism, institutional racism, and political naivete undercut the original vision of the Community Mental Health Act, resulting in huge service gaps to many people in need of mental health services, not just ethnic minority members.

Attempts under the Carter administration to address the unmet mental health needs of ethnic and racial minorities were undone by the Reagan administration, which introduced Mental Health Block Grant programs. This program essentially dismantled the federal role in organizing community mental health services. Although the National Institute for Mental Health could still fund innovative pilot programs to meet the needs of minorities, any follow-through was dependent on the political and economic whims of each state. In the budget-crisis atmosphere of the 1980s, most states saw revenues drop away for all social services. At the state level, many CMHCs cut back services to focus on care for only the mostly acutely or chronically mentally ill, thus limiting the options for meeting the outreach and prevention goals that had been identified for minority communities (Isaac & Armat, 1990; Vega & Murphy, 1990).

In states such as California, with swiftly growing multiethnic communities, meeting just the mental health needs of the most chronic or acutely mentally ill populations has meant addressing cross-cultural issues on various levels. In 1988, for example, ethnic minorities constituted a majority of patients in the state mental hospitals, were 54% of clients served by San Francisco county mental health programs, and were 38% of Santa Clara county's clients (California Association of Social Rehabilitation Agencies [CASRA], 1985; Ethnic Populations Services Planning Task Force, 1988; Nakao, 1990). One obvious inference to be drawn from these statistics is that all the mental health workers in these systems are working with culturally diverse clients. Another inference is that ethnic minorities are channeled at a high rate into public mental health programs, but whether this is because of lack of economic or geographic access to private services, or cultural reasons causing minorities to choose public services, or because of other dynamics, is unclear.

The same demographic changes in the state's population have affected other systems providing counseling and mental health services—the schools and the criminal justice system, for example. There has thus continued to be increasing pressure on all types of individual counselors and care-providing agencies to address multiculturalism. And, as pointed out by multicultural advocates (Highlen, 1994, 1996; Sue, 1994, 1995), a truly inclusive service delivery program can only occur in systemic changes of the very organizations that provide the services and that train mental health professions.

Lessons From Workforce Diversity Models

The attention that the counseling profession has paid to the development of multicultural competencies for individuals has gradually produced significant theoretical and practical suggestions, and attempts are clearly being made to integrate this knowledge into counselor training programs. To the degree that counselors do acquire multicultural counseling competency in training, however, the great majority of counseling professionals are employed by institutions or agencies that may not be capable of using an individual's multicultural competencies, or worse, may actually work against multicultural competencies and be oppressive to both culturally diverse staff and clients. It is essential that the development of individual skills be placed within a larger framework of organizational development if counseling and mental health organizations are to become truly multicultural.

Strangely, lessons on how an organization can become more culturally responsive can be found in the world of business and industry. Motivated by the statutory requirements of EEO and affirmative action policies on one hand, and by an acknowledgement of the changing demographics of the U.S. workforce on the other, organizational psychologists have begun to develop an approach to multicultural organizations frequently called "managing diversity," which is "conceptually different from equal employment opportunity, which was primarily a battle against racism and prejudice. To value workforce diversity is to manage in a way designed to seize the benefits that differences bring" (Copeland, 1988), and to embrace the idea that a multicultural or pluralistic environment is both inevitable and desirable.

Barr and Strong (1987) offer this general description of a multicultural organization:

> A multicultural organization is one that is genuinely committed to diverse representation of its membership; is sensitive to maintaining an open, supportive and responsive environment; is working toward and purposefully including elements of diverse cultures in its ongoing operations; and one that is authentic in its response to issues confronting it. (p. 20)

And they go on to note:

> To embrace multiculturalism means to think and behave differently and to change institutional policies. Any institution that takes this challenge genuinely is taking on years of struggle. (p. 23)

Schein (1990) reiterates the fact that major organizational change is a long and frequently arduous process. To begin the process, organizations must first understand their own culture before they can systematically adopt any new set of values and behaviors around issues as complex as racism, sexism, ethnocentrism, or other forms of discrimination.

All of the activities that revolve around recruitment, selection, training, socialization, the design of reward systems, the design and description of jobs, and the broader issues of organizational design require an understanding of how organizational culture influences present functioning. Many organizational change programs that failed probably did so because they ignored cultural forces in the organizations in which they were to be installed (p. 118).

Schein (1990) identifies three levels at which organizational culture manifests itself. The first level is that of artifacts: the physical environment, dress code, publications, products, and communication style of members. At the second level, he identifies values, norms, ideologies, and philosophies, but adds that to really understand an organizational culture, values must be understood within a third level, that of the assumptions that a culture's members make about the meaning of its values. These are often unconscious, but determine the perceptions, feelings, behavior, and thought processes of members. Schein compares the process of helping an organization come to understand its culture with that of the process of therapy for individuals, but notes that the "tactics are more complicated when multiple clients are involved and when some of the clients are groups and subsystems" (p. 117).

Just as the acquisition of individual multicultural awareness and competence is a complex developmental process with identifiable stages, organizational multicultural competence appears to be a similar developmental process (Adler, 1986; Sue, 1991a, 1995b). Before an organization can increase its multicultural competency, it is crucial to describe its current culture with regard to the dimensions identified by Sue et al. (1992), because each dimension represents either an obstacle to or an opportunity for change.

A number of researchers, working primarily from corporate models, have identified three general stages of organizational multicultural development that are fairly similar across models (see Table 8.1). Adler's (1986) model uses the terms Parochial, Ethnocentric, and Synergistic to describe an ascending scale of multicultural competency; Foster, Jackson, Cross, Jackson, and Hardiman (1988) use the terms Monocultural, Nondiscriminatory, and Multicultural to describe their scale.

The concern of these authors is to help business organizations understand that actively "managing diversity" allows organizations to "minimize the problems it causes while maximizing the advantages it allows" (Adler, 1986, p. 230). Motivation for an organization to change from one level to the next can come from internal forces, external pressures, or both, but in any case, organizations that acknowledge the full range of cultural diversity affecting them can turn this to their advantage while implementing change (Copeland, 1988).

Barr and Strong (1987), referring to attempts at multicultural development in university settings, describe three "models of program development in multiculturalism." They differentiate among programs motivated by a desire for interpersonal/attitudinal change (which they call the "liberal" intervention model), programs motivated by economic/behavioral concerns somewhat parallel to those characterized by the "managing diversity" model, and programs motivated by a desire for structural/behavioral changes, which they define as "radical," and as the only model that acknowledges the realities of institutional racism. Their criticisms would seem to imply that economic motivations may not be enough to bring about the "multicultural" or "synergistic" stages posited by other authors, if

Table 8.1 Stages of Multicultural Organizational Development

Author	Stages					
Adler (1986)	Parochial			Ethnocentric	Synergistic	
Foster, Jackson, Cross, Jackson, and Hardiman (1988)	Monocultural			Nondiscriminatory	Multicultural	
Barr and Strong (1987)	Traditional			Liberal, Managing Diversity	Radical	
Cross, Bazron, Dennis, and Isaacs (1989)	Cultural Destructiveness	Cultural Incapacity	Cultural Blindness	Cultural Precompetence	Cultural Competence	Cultural Proficiency
Characteristics typical of organizations at particular stages.	Cultural diversity is either deliberately ignored or destroyed. Organization members are monocultural or highly assimilated "tokens." Hiring practices are discriminatory, and services or products are inadequate or inappropriate for cultural minorities. Organizations believe there is only one right way to do things.		Organizations acknowledge that diversity exists and have "good intentions," but operate from a sense that "our way is the best way." Focus is on meeting affirmative action and EEO goals, with a legalistic approach to nondiscrimination. There may be attempts at cross-cultural sensitivity training for individuals, but no focus on organizational change. Staff may be culturally diverse but are judged by traditional (White, male) standards.		Organizations value diversity, view it as an asset rather than a problem. Staff diversity is evident at all levels, and staff are evaluated and promoted for meeting diversity criteria. Training focuses on the personal and organizational dynamics of racism, sexism, and so on. Planning is creative, flexible, to accomodate ongoing cultural change.	

substantial economic gain, workforce satisfaction, or both can be gained with less than radical changes.

Morrison and Von Glinow (1990), among others, have noted the phenomenon of the "glass ceiling" as indicative of institutional policies that embraced diversity only "so far," but they and other authors argue that the rapidly increasing number of women and minorities in the workforce, as well as the United States's need to compete in a global marketplace, will eventually force institutions to address multiculturalism at higher levels and, correspondingly, restructure themselves in ways that address all forms of institutional discrimination. To not do so will cause organizations to lose many skilled workers, who will prefer to work in organizations that value diversity, and will render businesses less able to compete in a multicultural marketplace (Copeland, 1988; Sue, 1991a; Thomas, 1990).

Many of the same motivations that are driving the development of multicultural business organizations apply to the predominately not-for-profit world of mental health, counseling agencies, and graduate training programs. To the degree that all nonprofits have needs to recruit, retain, and promote staff, and are legally accountable for various kinds of EEO and affirmative action practices, mental health agencies must consider goals toward a multicultural workforce. Instead of working for economic profit, however, mental health organizations are designed to provide community profit: supplying services that meet human needs. Instead of competing in a capitalistic marketplace, nonprofit organizations compete for funding from any combination of state, federal, county, or city agencies, and corporate, foundation, or individual charitable funds. Funding sources may impose a variety of objectives and restrictions on the money they offer, frequently as part of larger, politically motivated policies. To obtain funds, nonprofit counseling agencies may have to agree to target particular client groups or develop certain programs that match funders' goals, but do not represent the most crucial community needs. Nonprofit groups are, however, frequently in good positions to do the reverse: to identify community mental health needs, alert funding sources to their importance, and advocate for broader acknowledgement of the issues with increased funding and program development.

Culturally Competent Mental Health Organizations

The many issues identified in the earlier part of this book are among the motivations for mental health organizations to develop multiculturally competent organizations, the unmet needs of minority populations foremost among them. To meet those needs, a counseling organization must not only employ individuals with multicultural counseling skills, but the agency itself needs to have a "multicultural culture," if you will.

Alvarez et al. (1976) offer a general description of a mental health system that would meet community needs, including those of a multicultural population:

> A system that is more effective in reaching people and in allocating resources because of improved organization, redefined relationships, continued evaluation, and improved communications will be the hallmark of a functioning [health care] system. This can be successful only if the system's staff and board will engage in education of and by the community and its own affiliates for understanding the system and its potential. Comprehensive community mental health has value only if, beyond the concept, program implementation is compatible with the community's understanding of mental health and its interpretation of mental illness. There must be a meaningful relationship between the center's practices, consumers' problems, and community concerns. The programs and services must have the potential to provide solutions that the community accepts as valid. In the center's effort to respond to problems in subunits of a community, it must also explore the consequences of implementing a partial solution to a large community problem. (p. 69)

Cross, Bazron, Dennis, and Isaacs (1989) have incorporated the insights of many researchers and gone beyond the three-stage business models to describe a detailed, six-stage developmental continuum of cultural competence for care-giving organizations such as mental health agencies. These have been given the names (a) cultural destructiveness, (b) cultural incapacity, (c) cultural blindness, (d) cultural precompetence, (e) cultural competence, and (f) advocacy.

1. Cultural Destructiveness. Cross et al. (1989) acknowledge the checkered history of organizations and research ostensibly designed to "help" certain racial/ethnic groups by identifying the first stage of (in)competence as Cultural Destructiveness. This is represented by programs that have participated in culture/race-based oppression, forced assimilation, or even genocide. Historically, many federal government programs aimed at American Indians fit this description (Allen, 1986), as does the infamous Tuskegee experiment in which Black men with syphilis were deliberately left untreated (Sue & Sue, 1990), or Nazi-sponsored medical "experiments" that singled out Jews, Gypsies, gays/lesbians, and the disabled, among other groups, for systematic torture and death under the guise of medical research.

2. Cultural Incapacity. Cross et al.'s (1989) second stage is Cultural Incapacity, similar to Adler's (1986) Parochial and Foster et al.'s (1988) Monocultural stages. Organizations may not be intentionally culturally destructive, but lack the capacity to help minority clients or communities because the system remains extremely biased toward the racial/cultural superiority of the dominant group. The characteristics of cultural incapacity include: discriminatory hiring and other staffing practices; subtle messages to people of color that they are not valued or welcome, especially as manifested by environmental cues (building location, decoration, publicity that uses only Whites as models, and so on); and generally lower expectations of minority clients, based on unchallenged stereotypical beliefs.

3. Cultural Blindness. The third stage in Cross et al.'s (1989) continuum is one in which agencies provide services with the express philosophy that all people are the same, and the belief that helping methods used by the dominant culture are universally applicable. Despite the agency's good intentions, services are so ethnocentric as to make them inapplicable for all but the most assimilated minority group members. "Such services ignore cultural strengths, encourage assimilation, and blame the victim for their problems. . . . Outcome is usually measured by how closely a client approximates a middle-class, nonminority existence. Institutional racism restricts minority access to professional training, staff positions, and services" (Cross et al., p. 15). Foster et al.'s (1988) Nondiscriminatory stage fits here, and they note that organizations at this stage may have more of a fixation on "getting the numbers right" and eliminating any apparent signs of hostility toward new groups. Although there may be a sincere desire to eliminate a majority group's unfair advantages, the focus may end up on limited and legalistic attempts to comply with equal employment or affirmative action regulations. It is difficult for organizations to move past this stage if Whites or other cultural majority members are not willing to confront the ways they have benefited from institutional racism, and risk trying on new ways of sharing power (Barr & Strong, 1987).

4. Cultural Precompetence. Agencies at this stage have, as Schein (1990) might say, at least looked at the "artifacts" and values of their organization, to recognize their weaknesses in serving minorities and developing a multicultural staff. They may experiment with hiring more minority staff beyond the minimal numbers required to comply with EEO goals, may recruit minorities for boards of directors or advisory committees, might work cooperatively to perform needs assessments with minority groups in their service area, and institute cultural sensitivity training for staff, including management. They may propose new programs specifically for a particular ethnic/cultural group, but if planning is not done carefully, this program may end up marginalized within the agency.

It is at this stage that the level of individuals' racial/ethnic identity awareness comes more clearly to the forefront, where individuals who are less aware of their stage of development may remain unchallenged within a system that overall is pleased with its accomplishments. "One danger at this level is a false sense of accomplishment or of failure that prevents the agency from moving forward along the continuum. . . . Another danger is tokenism" (Cross et al., 1989, p. 16) in which minority professionals are expected to raise the agency's level of cross-cultural efficacy by simply being present in slightly greater numbers. Minority staff may lack training, however, in many of the skills or knowledge areas that would allow them to translate their personal experience into effective counseling, not to mention training of coworkers.

If the task of developing cultural awareness has been given to minority staff (or motivated majority staff) who do not have the clout to involve all elements of the agency, "this pattern of program development allows for the phony embracing of multiculturalism because the dominant group can remain on the sidelines judging programs and helping the institution to continue on its merry way" (Barr & Strong, 1987, p. 21). These staff may sacrifice job performance in other areas and then be criticized, or work doubly hard because of taking on the extra burden of cultural awareness activities, and then may not receive any acknowledgment, in patterns that continue the oppression of minorities (Gallegos, 1982).

5. Cultural Competence. Agencies at this stage show "continuing self-assessment regarding culture, careful attention to the dynamics of difference, continuous expansion of cultural knowledge and resources, and a variety of adaptations to service models to better meet the needs" of culturally diverse populations" (p. 17).

Organizations at this stage will have a diverse staff at all levels, and most individuals will have reached the higher stages of individual racial/cultural identity awareness: aware of and able to articulate their cultural identity, values, and attitudes toward cultural diversity issues. This will be true for both majority and minority culture members. Staff will regularly be offered or seek out opportunities to increase their cross-cultural skills and knowledge. There is recognition that minority group members have to be at least bicultural in U.S. society, and that this creates its own mental health issues concerning identity, assimilation, values conflicts, and so on, for staff as well as clients. There will be enough multilingual staff available to offer clients choices in relating to service providers. If the agency has culture-specific programs under its umbrella, these programs are perceived by agency staff and clients as integral to the agency, and not just "junior partners."

6. *Cultural Proficiency*. This stage encompasses the highest goals of Adler's (1986) Synergistic and Foster et al.'s (1988) Multicultural stages. As Adler notes, these organizations are very uncommon, given that both the organizational culture and individuals within it are operating at high levels of multicultural competence, having overcome many layers of racism, prejudice, discrimination, and ignorance.

Organizations at this stage seek to add to the knowledge base of culturally competent practices by "conducting research, developing new therapeutic approaches based on culture, and disseminating the results of demonstration projects" (Cross et al., 1989, p. 17), and follow through on their "broader social responsibility to fight social discrimination and advocate social diversity" in all forums (Foster et al., 1988, p. 3).

Staff are hired who are specialists in culturally competent practices, or are trained and supervised systematically to reach competency. Every level of an agency (board members, administrators, counselors, and consumers) regularly participates in evaluations of the agency's cross-cultural practices and environment, and are able to articulate the agency's values and strategies concerning cultural diversity. If the agency runs culture-specific programs, these programs are used as resources for everyone in the agency and community, and not perceived as belonging just to that ethnic community (Munoz & Sanchez, 1996).

9

Multicultural Organizational Development

Evolving Toward Organizational Cultural Competence

MULTICULTURAL COUNSELING COMPETENCE IS . . .

- Being able to identity the major characteristics of the multiculturally competent organization:
    Values diversity
    Possesses the capacity for self-assessment or cultural auditing
    Clarifies its visions
    Understands dynamics of difference
    Institutionalizes cultural knowledge
    Adapts to diversity
- Planning for organizational cultural competency via:
    Assessments
    Cultivates support
    Develops leadership
    Develops multicultural policies
    Implements

Describing a continuum of competence is not the same as identifying the methods by which organizations reach new levels of competence. Having identified themselves on the continuum, how do organizations, particularly mental health agencies and counselor training programs, actually reach higher levels of multicultural competence? Drawing on the insights of various authors (Copeland, 1988; Cross, Bazron, Dennis, & Isaacs, 1989; Gallegos, 1982; Jensen, 1992; Munoz & Sanchez, 1996; Sue, 1991a; Thomas, 1990), at least six elements appear to be essential to an organization's ability to offer a multiculturally competent system of mental health care or education. They are similar to the elements required of individuals in that they include attitudes/beliefs, worldviews, and specific abilities. The multiculturally competent mental health organization will possess the following characteristics.

1. Values diversity: An organization will respect and value the fact that its personnel and its clients come from very different backgrounds, and that communication styles, behaviors, values, and attitudes will legitimately vary concerning the provision of mental health services and training. There will be an appreciation of diversity within cultures as well as between them, and White Euro-Americans will be understood as just one equally valuable group among peers, rather than the model against which other groups are judged.

2. Possesses a capacity for cultural self-assessment or cultural auditing: Leaders in the agency or training program will understand that their system has been shaped by culture, has its own "culture," and will be able to assess how their system interacts with and is different from other cultures. Because this process can often threaten people's power or sense of identity, and because it involves looking at a body of (usually) unspoken and unexamined assumptions, and values, it is likely that outside consultants will be needed, although Thomas (1990) is more emphatic, asserting that it "is impossible to conduct a cultural audit without outside help" (p. 114). Services, products, and processes may all be assessed, along with the physical and larger political environments.

3. Clarifies its visions: Everyone in an agency will have a good idea of the goals of the organization, both in terms of multiculturalism and types of mental health services and training to be provided. Members of a multicultural task force looking at services for ethnic populations in Santa Clara county (California) were asked to "dream" about what the ideal mental health system would look like for their respective communities, then develop goals and strategies for reaching their dream. The clarifying question was: "Would my mother, grandfather, sister, or brother use the services as they currently exist? What would it take to have them walk into the doors of a mental health services setting?" (Ethnic Populations Services Planning Task Force, 1988, p. 1).

4. Understands the dynamics of difference: Agency leaders or university administrators will have specific knowledge concerning the dynamics that occur when two or more groups confront stereotypes, political and power differences, and the histories of misinterpretation and misjudgment that combine in expressions of racism, sexism, or other forms of discrimination.

Sue (1991a) emphasizes that "any multicultural training program must ultimately contain a strong antiracism component" (p. 104), and leaders must be prepared for resistances to this. In addition, leaders will have a good understanding of the overall dynamics of change: These dynamics are the reason people resist most major changes and leaders will need strategies to address this (see Jaffe, 1982 and Spaniol, Zipple, & Cohen, 1990 for complete discussions). Agencies will be able to work creatively and flexibly to negotiate trust and cooperation among culturally diverse constituencies, including their own staffs. Finally, when exploring cultural differences, people will be helped to understand that they are "change agents," and in many cases, pioneers—it is to be expected that they will make mistakes while exploring new territory (Thomas, 1990).

5. Institutionalizes its cultural knowledge: An organization will have systems and methods commonly used at all levels for personnel to acquire and make use of cultural knowledge. For example, board members, directors, or university administrators may have systematic links to culturally diverse community groups; supervisors and instructors are able to provide cross-cultural supervision or multicultural education; counselors are able to solicit and make use of culturally related feedback from their clients; and, awareness of cultural issues is documented in all the written materials and records of the agency. Cross-cultural issues are routinely included in case presentations, and there is a library of relevant multicultural references. Agencies advocate with local governments for the accurate collect on of community demographics.

6. Adapts to diversity: It is understood that multiculturalism is an ever-changing process, so new programs or interventions will continue to be developed, staff will be hired, or other community resources will be promoted to help meet the needs of new groups who should be served under an organization's mandate. This may well mean adopting new ideas of what constitutes "mental health" services or multicultural education, and incorporating models from other cultures—use of traditional healers and folk remedies, for example, or greater involvement of families or other support networks (Lefley, 1990). Each population will be evaluated for its particular needs: An example of this comes from Santa Clara county, where a mental health task force from the African American, Asian American, and Hispanic American communities made six recommendations for service changes that applied to all their communities, three recommendations that were shared by two of the groups, and seven recommendations that were specific to one community (Ethnic Populations Services Planning Task Force, 1988).

Planning for Cultural Competency

Agencies and training institutions interested in increasing multiculturalism will serve themselves best by planning as carefully as possible; yet, the many issues related to a minority mental health perspective or multicultural education threaten to overwhelm even the most conscientious of administrators or educators (Gallegos, 1982, p. 96). Although changes in an organization's cultural competency may occur by plan or happenstance, planned change is usually perceived as desired change, whereas unplanned changes are more likely to cause confusion and resistance (Spaniol et al., 1990).

Gowdy and Rapp's study (as cited in Spaniol et al., 1990, p. 29) identified change as one of the main characteristics of a quality mental health organization. Specifically, a quality program is responsive to consumer needs and wants, promotes the health and well-being of staff members, is responsive to funding sources, is open to change and growth in all areas and plans for it, and facilitates leadership development within all members. Within this framework of change, the process of planning for cultural diversity is a broad one, as suits an issue of great scope and complexity. The process involves assessment, building support, facilitating leadership, developing policies, and implementing change.

Initial Assessment

Morrison and Von Glinow (1990) suggest that assessments for "remedial action" take into account three areas: "human capital," or the education and recruitment of employees; types of discriminatory treatment; and structural and contextual barriers to cultural diversity. Sue (1991a) has offered a comprehensive conceptual framework for the assessment of organization's multicultural competency. His model for cultural diversity assessment and training provides a structure for Morrison and Von Glinow's observations, and expands on Schein's (1990) three levels of organizational culture to look at them from three perspectives: levels of organizational intervention, barriers to multicultural change, and ways of incorporating multicultural competencies into organizations. More specifically, Sue has designed a "3 × 3 × 3 matrix, which analyzes an organization's functional focus (recruitment, retention, and promotion); barriers (differences, discrimination, and systemic factors); and cross-cultural competencies (beliefs/attitudes, knowledge, and skills)" (p. 99) (see Figures 9.1 and 9.2).

The first step for any organization must be a cultural assessment, which should reveal the barriers to and resources available for making changes. Using a framework like Sue's (1991a), it is possible for an organization to assess multiple levels of its operations, to target specific areas for change, and to develop interventions appropriate to a particular area. Many authors have offered suggestions likely to be helpful to planners during the assessment process, when considered from a multicultural perspective (Cross

FUNCTIONAL LEVELS	Differences	BARRIERS		
		Interpersonal Discrimination	Systemic Barriers	
Recruitment (labor pool)	Effectiveness training for minorities and majority individuals	• Consciousness raising • Sensitivity training • Increased knowledge • Cross-cultural management skills	• Organizational development • Systems intervention • Creating new programs and practices	
Retention (corporate culture)	Effectiveness training for minorities and majority individuals	• Consciousness raising • Sensitivity training • Increased knowledge • Cross-cultural management skills	• Organizational development • Systems intervention • Creating new programs and practices	
Promotion/ Advancement (career path)	Effectiveness training for minorities and majority individuals	• Consciousness raising • Sensitivity training • Increased knowledge • Cross-cultural management skills	• Organizational development • Systems intervention • Creating new programs and practices	

Figure 9.1. Cultural Diversity Training: A Systemic Approach

NOTE: Developed by Derald Wing Sue Ph.D. A Psychological Corporation (not to be reproduced without written permission).

et al., 1989; Gallegos, 1982; Munoz & Sanchez, 1996; Schein, 1990; Spaniol et al., 1991; Sue, 1991b; Thomas, 1990):

1. Have the support of agency leadership to do the assessment.
2. Assess the administrative or educational style, including how and by whom decisions are made and transmitted—is it an autocratic, democratic, or consensual style?
3. Have a realistic sense of the planners' own power to influence the agency's or training environment, get issues on the agenda.
4. Know which people, both in and outside the agency or university, can be counted on to promote change, and include them in the process.
5. Be familiar with any other assessment processes previously used by the organization, or related organizations; evaluate them, and make use of them if appropriate for reasons of efficiency, and consistency.

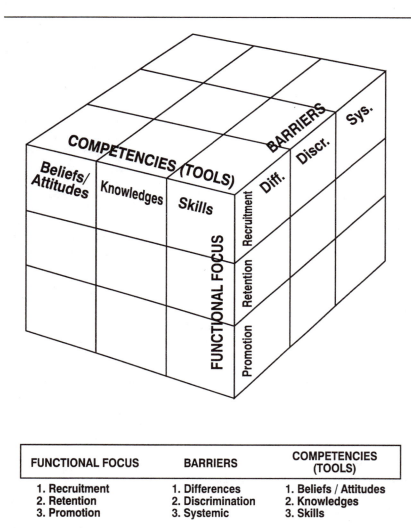

FUNCTIONAL FOCUS	BARRIERS	COMPETENCIES (TOOLS)
1. Recruitment	1. Differences	1. Beliefs / Attitudes
2. Retention	2. Discrimination	2. Knowledges
3. Promotion	3. Systemic	3. Skills

Figure 9.2. A Model for Cultural Diversity Training

NOTE: Developed by Derald Wing Sue, Ph.D., A Psychological Corporation (not to be reproduced without written permission).

6. Understand which sections of the agency or university must be most affected to bring about the desired change, which people are involved, and how best to approach those different areas and people effectively.

7. Present the assessment in a positive light, as a means for identifying areas for growth, rather than a vehicle for criticism.

8. Anticipate that there will be problems during the assessment, and leave the process flexible enough to accommodate change.

Cultivating Support

After assessing the readiness and resources available for change, planners should make sure they have cultivated support for their cultural competency goals. The planners should be sure that they understand the types of information that people inside the agency or university and outside in the community both need to be helpful. Procedures that planners may wish to follow include the following:

1. Initiating, in key settings, discussions of the values and principles of the agency or educational institution, as they relate to multiculturalism. Articulating these in positive, constructive ways will help build support from those present.

2. Involving, or at minimum, informing, all levels of the organization about the issues, so that a "critical mass" of people reach consensus that cultural competency is indeed a priority for the agency, and these people have a sense of "ownership" of the issues.

3. Making allies within the larger community—business, religious, political or cultural groups, and the media—which can help the community have an impact on the agency or university environment. This might also include working with mental health-specific advocacy and consumer groups.

Developing Leadership

The initial impetus for developing cultural competence may come from any level within an organization: top leadership, entry-level staff, staff of particular racial/ethnic or gender groups; or from without the organization, in the form of political, legal, or economic pressures. Research strongly suggests, however, that no comprehensive implementation of multicultural practices can take place without the support of top decision- and policy-makers in the organization, of whatever cultural background (Morrison & Van Glinow, 1990; Schein, 1990). Equally important for the long-term success of multiculturalism is the development of leadership that is multiculturally diverse, as well as being competent to implement multicultural policies—in other words, diversity must be combined with institutional policies that value diversity.

Those planners hoping to increase an organization's cultural competency must pay particular attention to leadership development, both formal and informal. Because multiculturalism is an issue that touches almost everyone in our society on a personal level, it may inspire the work of many informal leaders in organizations, who speak up in concern for their cultural "community," be that a culture based on ethnicity, race, religion, sexual preference, or any other shared identity. Within a mental health agency, acceptance and support for multiculturalistic changes may rest as strongly on informal leadership as it does on formal leadership, and planners will profit if they understand this as a strength (Cross et al., 1989; Gallegos, 1982; Munoz & Sanchez, 1996).

On a formal level, however, leadership for cultural diversity begins with recruitment of a diverse staff, who are then consistently assessed and evaluated in ways that consciously recognize the strengths and weaknesses involved in their cultural style. For example, the experience an Asian American female might bring in harmonious conflict resolution and consensual decision making is considered equally as valuable as a White male's experience in more assertive or hierarchical decision-making styles (Sue & Sue, 1990).

Not only are staff members' existing cultural styles of communication and leadership acknowledged, but the requirement for multicultural leadership development within mental health organizations specifically requires that all staff be assessed for their multicultural counseling competencies, as described earlier in this book. Integral to the development of these competencies is the development of an individual's own sense of ethnic/racial identity, one's knowledge of one's own values and worldview, and an awareness of the attitudes and assumptions one brings to cross-cultural encounters. Therefore, leadership development will include training and assessment across these issues.

Mentorship has been identified as one of the most important mechanisms by which employees are initiated into organizational culture and groomed for leadership roles (Redmond, 1990; Schein, 1990). Morrison and Von Glinow (1990) reviewed the literature on mentorship, and concluded that within predominantly White male-dominated business environments, mentor relationships "are harder to manage and provide a narrower range of benefits for women and minorities" (p. 203). Issues contributing to this include the fact that mentors are most likely to mentor people with whom they identify, usually people of the same race/ethnicity and gender (Redmond, 1990); and cross-race relationships usually take longer to develop and are subject to social scrutiny, whereas cross-gender relationships are subject to sexual innuendo. Morrison and Von Glinow (1990) state that the literature suggests that cultural minority employees may need more mentors or sponsors than do cultural majority employees: a majority-culture mentor to initiate them into the organizational culture, and a same-culture mentor to increase their comfort and security level.

There is disagreement about the efficacy of leadership training programs that target one particular cultural (gender, ethnicity, language) group. Thomas (1990) suggests that organizations apply the "special consideration test" to all such training programs, and ask "Will it contribute to everyone's success, or will it only produce an advantage for Blacks or Whites or women or men? Is it designed for them as opposed to us? Whenever the answer is yes, you're not yet on the road to managing diversity" (p. 117). Thomas offers the example of a company in which the problem identified was that Blacks were not moving up. The company eventually identified the reason as poor supervision and professional development practices that were affecting everyone, even White males, in negative ways, and so a solution focusing just on Blacks would have been incomplete. Thomas acknowledges, however, that there may be barriers caused by actual discrimination, and that these might need to be addressed with affirmative action remedies.

Morrison and Von Glinow (1990) emphasize that organizations need to be flexible in considering different types of leadership training, because some minorities will find the idea of segregated programs offensive. They cite research that shows that in organizations in which there are only token levels of minorities, those minorities may be expected to have advanced levels of certain skills. Specifically, African Americans may be expected to manage conflicts very quickly, and to be skilled at managing racist incidents, as well as their own rage over the racism they encounter (Dickens & Dickens, 1982, as cited in Morrison & Von Glinow, 1990). Knowing this, African Americans who do not feel their organization is able or willing to implement systemwide cultural awareness or conflict-resolution training may want to organize their own training on these issues, for example, to enhance their status within an ethnocentric environment.

Developing Multicultural Policies

The most important factor in designing policies that are truly multicultural is the involvement of all community members who might possibly be affected (Cross et al., 1989; Gallegos, 1982; Munoz & Sanchez, 1996). Increasingly, for mental health organizations and university based-training programs, this means including not just counseling providers and community leaders, but consumers as well (California Association of Social

Rehabilitation Agencies [CASRA], 1985; Golden, 1992). In California, a 1984 law requires that primary consumers (not just parents or family members) be included on all county mental health advisory boards (Golden, 1992).

Because virtually all mental health organizations espouse a desire for diversity, and because most organizations that receive any public funding are mandated to provide services to underrepresented populations, there are plenty of macrolevel policies in place to motivate organizations to reach the superficial levels of cultural competency (CASRA, 1985). As has been previously discussed, however, policies mean little if organizations maintain ethnocentric practices that alienate culturally diverse staff and clients alike.

Therefore, some more specific strategies for developing policies to develop multicultural competence include the following:

1. Recruitment of large numbers, a critical mass, of culturally diverse community leaders to serve on boards, task forces, or advisory committees, so that representation goes beyond token levels.

2. The development of cross-cultural representation and proficiency standards by governing or licensing bodies, or professional organizations (CASRA, 1985; Sue, Arredondo, & McDavis, 1992) that require continuing education and evidence of compliance, not just at one time.

3. Organization training policies that support or even require participation by all personnel in training that builds cultural knowledge, skills, and aptitudes. Of course, an organization must commit the resources to implement such training, and have the capacity to assess the worth of training resources (Cross et al., 1989; Munoz & Sanchez, 1996).

4. Adopting decision-making policies that systematically solicit and encourage minority participation at all levels of the organization.

5. Seeking funding sources that support or require the development of multicultural competencies and services (or educating funding sources about the need for such programs!)

6. Incorporating cultural competency development into the written mission statement and goals of an agency, for example, in a 5-year plan. The process should be divided into manageable parts, with reasonable timelines, and the competencies should be spelled out (Cross et al., 1989). In addition, as any one policy of an agency is examined or revised, it should be studied for its impact on service delivery to culturally diverse populations, as well as for the impact on recruiting and promoting culturally diverse staff. Individuals within the agency are made accountable for identifying policy implications and implementing the identified goals.

Implementation

It is at the administrative level that policy may not only be created, but is interpreted and implemented on a daily basis. Thus, individuals taking the lead in helping an agency reach cultural proficiency must be able to use its administrative procedures effectively. Strategies supporting administrative cultural competency include the following:

1. Collecting demographic data that allows the agency or training program to evaluate the cultural make-up of its staff, clientele, and community, and to know whether the agency is representative of the community (Cross et al., 1989; Ethnic Populations Services Planning Task Force, 1988; Munoz & Sanchez, 1996).

2. Developing staff recruitment policies and procedures that ensure that all communities are made aware of employment opportunities, that the skills and experiences of culturally diverse applicants are evaluated in ways that acknowledge and respect differences, and that cultural competence is addressed specifically in job descriptions. These procedures are in addition to affirmative action policies, and may include asking questions in the interview process about cultural diversity issues, requiring cross-cultural experience, or encouraging applicants with non-Eurocentric, culturally based counseling/healing experiences (Copeland, 1988; Lefley, 1990; Munoz & Sanchez, 1996; Sue, 1991a).

3. Designing administrative forms and procedures, such as staff orientations, program evaluations, client intake forms, case note formats, and so on, in such a way that cultural diversity issues are actively solicited and included in the procedures (Munoz & Sanchez, 1996).

4. Designing educational materials and agency literature that acknowledges the particular concerns of various communities, and that is available in clients' primary languages.

5. Developing staff training and supervision programs that focus not only on the acquisition of cultural knowledge, but also on the sociopolitical dynamics of diversity, and that make use of up-to-date research and community resources (Cross et al., 1989).

6. Developing personnel policies that are culturally sensitive; for example, having personal leave time that can be used to accommodate cultural differences in holidays or community events, or advocating for medical plans that cover "nontraditional therapies," such as acupuncture (Sue, Ivey, & Pedersen, 1996).

7. Familiarizing all staff with information concerning the appropriate use of translators, and providing support for and developing training programs for nonprofessional staff or community members who are frequently used as translators.

Administrative staff will have opportunities to work with boards, advisory committees, funding sources, and other community groups in designing mental health programs that address the needs of multicultural populations. Although specific program design is beyond the scope of this book, certain basic areas of multicultural awareness and competence should be mentioned under the implementation focus:

1. Making sure that programs are geographically accessible and physically attractive to target populations.
2. Offering services that can include all the relevant members of a client's support system—family, extended family, spiritual leaders, and so forth.

Conclusion

It is unlikely that the completely multiculturally competent mental health organization or educational program exists, or may ever exist, given the multiple dimensions of knowledge, resources, and action involved. But there is no question that there is tremendous room for improvement in existing programs, as well as the need for more and innovative mental health services for all Americans (Cross et al., 1989; Ethnic Populations Services Planning Task Force, 1988; Isaac & Arnat, 1990). A truly multiculturally competent mental health and counseling service needs to infuse multiculturalism at the policy-making level, administrative level, and service level. The same statement is applicable to all psychology training programs and to our professional organizations as well.

The trend toward multiculturally competent mental health services and multicultural education has many contributing factors. Demographic changes, political and legal requirements, developments in counseling theory and practice, and new models of organizational development can all play roles in helping mental health services become effective multicultural models for other institutions.

Although no counseling or mental health service or training program can ever claim to meet the needs of all of its clients/students, or fully use every skill of its employees, it is clear that counselors, educators, and programs are much more likely to be successful when they are aware of and prepared to address the multicultural dimensions of their environment, and to address complex issues of racism and other forms of discrimination. At the same time, understanding the universal aspects of culture and cultural identity development can help all counselors and teachers to better understand even culturally similar clients/students, as well as helping organizations to more effectively recruit, support, and promote the broadest range of employees.

Because of the particular attributes involved in counseling—self-awareness, empathy, good communication skills, the desire to help others—members of the counseling profession are among those people best suited for the task of modeling and teaching multicultural skills. Similarly, mental health organizations should be able to model the planning and development processes involved in responding to complex human needs. Yet neither individuals nor organizations can approach multiculturalism without a solid understanding of the conceptual frameworks on which such a complex structure is built.

By combining the work of those researchers who have identified individual multicultural counseling competencies, and those who have described the multiculturally competent organization, it is our hope that anyone involved in providing mental health services can identify multiple directions in which she or he can find a sense of efficacy and inspiration, while living and working in an increasingly multicultural world.

10

Implementing Personal,
Professional, and Organizational
Multicultural Competence

MULTICULTURAL COUNSELING
COMPETENCE IS . . .

- Being able to develop experiences related to personal multicultural competence:

    Obtain a balanced and realistic picture of racial/ethnic minority groups

    Enlist the help of a cultural guide

    Read literature written by or for persons of the culture

    Attend cultural events, meetings, and community forums

    Learn to ask sensitive racial questions

    Tune in to your feelings and emotions related to race issues, situations, or both

- Being able to develop experiences related to professional multicultural competence.

- Being able to develop and propose strategies for organizational multicultural competence:

    For graduate schools of counseling and clinical psychology it involves a systemic analysis of the following areas: (a) student and faculty multicultural competence, (b) curriculum infusion, (c) diversity representation, (d) therapeutic practice and supervision, (e) research, (f) support services, and (g) programs, policies, and structures.

Becoming a multiculturally competent mental health professional, educator, administrator, or member of society requires a constant and ongoing commitment to change as it relates to awareness, knowledge, and skills. This change must occur in three contexts: personal, professional, and organizational (Toporek & Reza, 1994). Throughout this text, we have attempted to build a case for both professional and institutional change. Yet, examination of multicultural competencies is not adequate if only professional aspects of the person are considered, whereas personal and deeply held beliefs are not addressed. Although all three contexts are interrelated, it may be helpful to discuss them separately and suggest what mental health professionals and educators can do at each level of analysis. Some examples of cultural competence development are given next; however, they are far from exhaustive.

Personal Multicultural Competence

At the end of a course or workshop on multiculturalism, participants often express not only satisfaction with the experience, but also dissatisfaction. They are likely to complain that the training barely touched on the issues, that much more needs to be done, that the university should offer more courses on multicultural psychology, and that there is a need for the instructors to be more confrontive with participants about their biases and prejudices. Although these complaints are legitimate and justified, participants may fail to see the erroneous assumptions being made: (a) Racism and prejudice reduction is solely the responsibility of the training program; and (b) A person can become multiculturally competent simply by taking coursework. As we have repeatedly emphasized, becoming multiculturally competent and sensitive is more than an intellectual exercise and the responsibility for change resides strongly in the individual as well. Further, to believe that 5 to 6 years of graduate training (no matter how multicultural the program) can easily overcome the years of negative cultural conditioning is simply not realistic.

Although many of us are willing to acknowledge that racism, sexism, homophobia, and other biases must be addressed at a professional and institutional level, we often avoid addressing these on a personal level and fail to identify personal growth as a necessary element for competence in multicultural counseling (Toporek & Reza, 1994). Some would argue that it is difficult, if not impossible, for a mental health professional to be multiculturally competent without understanding and working through their own personal biases and prejudices (Cheatham, 1994; Ibrahim, 1991;

Toporek & Reza, 1994). They emphasize that cultural competence must entail a willingness to address internal issues related to personal belief systems, behaviors, and emotions when interacting with culturally different individuals. There must be a personal awakening and a willingness to "root out" biases and unwarranted assumptions related to race, culture, ethnicity, and so on. When confronting racism on a personal level, several assumptions can guide our personal actions (Jones, 1997; Sherover-Marcuse, 1994):

1. No one was born wanting to be "racist," "sexist," or "homophobic." No one was born with racist attitudes and beliefs. Misinformation related to culturally different groups is not acquired by our free choice. These are imposed through a painful process of social conditioning; one is taught to hate and fear others who are different in some way.
2. Having racist attitudes and beliefs is harmful not only to persons of color, but to White Euro-Americans as well. It serves as a clamp on one's mind, distorting the perception of reality. It allows Whites to misperceive themselves as superior and all other groups to be inferior. It allows for the systematic mistreatment of large groups of people based on misinformation.
3. People of color grow up in an environment in which they, too, acquire misinformation about themselves and about Whites. They may come to believe in the inferiority of their group and themselves, or they may become unable to separate their oppressive experiences from accurate information about White people.
4. Becoming multiculturally competent means that we must overcome the inertia and feeling of powerlessness on a personal level. People can grow and change if they are personally willing to confront and unlearn their racist and sexist conditioning. To accomplish this task, we must unlearn racist misinformation not only on a cognitive (factual) level, but the misinformation that has been glued together by painful emotions must be dealt with affectively as well. We must begin to accept the responsibility for the pain and suffering we may have personally caused others.

Unlearning our biases means acquiring accurate information and experiences. Much of how we come to know about other cultures is through the media, what our family and friends convey to us, and through public education texts. These sources cannot be counted on to give an accurate picture because they can be filled with stereotypes, misinformation, and deficit portrayals. For psychologists, we are especially prone to distortions about cultural groups because our work deals with troubled people. When one is constantly exposed to troubled families in a particular cultural group, learning about the strengths and beauty of the culture becomes difficult. Thus, four principles can guide us in obtaining an accurate picture of culturally different groups. First, we must experience and learn from as many sources as possible (not just the media or what our neighbor may say) to check out the validity of our understanding. Second, a balanced picture of any group requires that we spend time with healthy and strong people of that culture. Third, we must supplement our factual under-standing with the experiential reality of the groups we hope to understand. Last, our lives must become a "have to" in being constantly vigilant to manifestations of bias in both ourselves and in the people around us. Some helpful suggestions for the personal unlearning of racist beliefs, attitudes, and behaviors are given next (Cross, 1995/1996; McIntosh, 1989; Sherover-Marcuse, 1994; Winter, 1977). Although these suggestions relate specifi-cally to racism, they apply to biases directed at other oppressed groups as well.

1. A balanced picture of racial/ethnic minority groups must come from spending time with healthy representatives of that culture. The mass media and our educational texts (written from the perspectives of Euro-Americans) fre-quently portray minority groups as uncivilized, pathological, criminals, or delinquents. No wonder the images we have are primarily negative. We must individually make an effort to fight such negative conditioning and ask our-selves what are the desirable aspects of the culture, the history, and the people.

2. Identify a cultural guide—someone from the culture who is willing to help you understand his or her group; someone willing to introduce you to new experiences; someone willing to help you process your thoughts, feelings, and behaviors. This allows you to more easily obtain valid information on race and racism issues.

3. Read literature written by or for persons of the culture. This applies to both fiction and nonfiction. Although the professional and nonprofessional litera-ture often portrays minorities in stereotypic ways, writings from individuals of that group may provide a richness based on experiential reality. Such an approach may make it possible to enter the culture in a safe, nonthreatening way. Other sources of information include minority-run or minority-edited radio and TV stations or publications.

4. Attend cultural events, meetings, and activities of the group. This allows you to view the people interacting in their community and observe their values in action. Hearing from church leaders, attending open community forums, and attending community celebrations allows you to sense the strengths of the community, observe leadership in action, personalizes your understanding, and allows you to identify potential guides and advisers.

5. Learn how to ask sensitive racial questions from your minority friends, associates, and acquaintances. Persons subjected to racism seldom get a

chance to talk about it with an undefensive and nonguilty person from the majority group. Whites, for example, often avoid mentioning race even with close minority friends. Most minority individuals are more than willing to respond, to enlighten and to share, if they sense that your questions and concerns are sincere and motivated by a desire to learn and serve the group. When a White person listens undefensively, for example, to a Black person speak about racism, both gain.

6. Tune in to your feelings and emotions when race-related issues or racial situations present themselves. Feelings of uneasiness, differentness, or outright fear when around persons of color are very meaningful. They may reveal or say something about your biases and prejudices. Do not make excuses for them, dismiss them, or avoid attaching some meaning to these thoughts and feelings. Only if we confront them directly, can they be unlearned or dealt with in a realistic manner.

7. Finally, dealing with racism, sexism, and homophobia means a personal commitment to action. It means interrupting other Whites when they make racist remarks, jokes, or engage in racist actions even if this is embarrassing or frightening. It means noticing the possibility for direct action against bias and discrimination in your everyday life—in the family, work, and the community. For persons of color, dealing with bias and prejudice is a day-to-day occurrence. If White folks are to be helpful, their lives must also be a constant "have to be" in dealing with racism.

Professional Multicultural Competence

Most of what we have discussed in the other chapters, touches on our role as a mental health practitioner in a professional context. We have stressed the need for counselors and therapists to acquire the awareness, knowledge, and skills needed for working effectively with culturally different clients. Specifically, these include the following:

1. *Recognizing that conventional mental health practice is culture-bound and reflects a Euro-American worldview.* This is first and foremost for the counselor or therapist. It may or may not be applicable to a culturally different client; when not, the danger of cultural oppression is ever present.

2. *Acquiring culture-specific information about the life experiences, values, assumptions, and histories of culturally different groups in society.* This becomes especially important if your clientele is racially and culturally diverse.

3. *Understanding yourself as a racial/cultural being and the potential impact it might have in the therapeutic relationship.* Whether you are a counselor with a Euro-American, Asian American, or African American background, will affect how you perceive the world and may affect how your client views you.

4. *Being able to use culturally relevant intervention strategies means breaking away from the narrow confines imposed via encapsulation.* Expanding the repertoire of helping responses to include traditionally taboo behaviors (giving advice and suggestions, counselor self disclosure, and so on) becomes a necessity in effective multicultural counseling.

5. *Playing alternative helping roles besides the conventional counselor or therapist ones maximizes the chances of providing appropriate services to culturally different clients.* Being an adviser, consultant, change agent, or facilitator of indigenous helping resources may prove more beneficial to some groups than traditional counseling.

6. *Acknowledging, respecting, and using non-Western indigenous healing methods and approaches means offering culturally relevant services to an increasingly diverse society and global world.* Becoming increasingly holistic, acknowledging the existence of spirituality, and using psychoeducational helping emphases recognizes the totality of the human condition.

Professional multicultural development may be attained through continuing education workshops, formal multicultural coursework, forming liaisons with the minority community, volunteering time to work in community mental health centers, reading the writings and research of minority scholars and mental health practitioners, and practicing the suggestions given for personal multicultural competence development. Above all, professional multicultural development demands an active learning process at the cognitive, affective, and behavioral levels. It means critically deconstructing the counseling/therapy literature, assumptions, theories, and practices of our profession.

Organizational Multicultural Competence

In Chapters 8 and 9, we spent considerable time discussing multicultural organizational development and the lessons gleaned from the community mental health movement, business and industry, and mental health delivery systems. As professional organizations (the American Psychological Association and the American Counseling Association) and graduate schools in counseling and clinical psychology represent organizational entities, the same characteristics of becoming multiculturally responsive seem to apply. Although it would be very beneficial to discuss how to make the APA and ACA more culturally inclusive, we have chosen to concentrate this last section on an example of affecting change in a graduate training program. We believe that multicultural organizational development principles may be applied to any institutional entity.

Multicultural Organizational Development (MOD) and Graduate Training

A decade and a half ago, Copeland (1982) highlighted the need for multicultural training in counseling programs and described four approaches or methods for multicultural implementation. The four approaches were the Separate Course model, the Area of Concentration model, the Interdisciplinary model, and the Integration model. The Separate Course model involves adding a multicultural course to the existing curriculum. Extending the single-course approach, the area of concentration model includes a core of courses that usually include skill-building activities and practicums. The Interdisciplinary model involves taking culture-focused courses outside one's program in such disciplines as anthropology, sociology, economics, and ethnic studies. This model provides for a broadened theoretical base with regard to multicultural issues. Finally, the integration model involves infusing multicultural issues into all courses and training experiences. Copeland (1982) discusses implementation requirements for each method and describes the advantages and disadvantages of each approach.

Like many of the models of business and industry, D'Andrea and Daniels (1991) assessed the status of multicultural training and proposed a developmental framework to classify current training programs. The authors describe a two-level, four-stage framework. Level 1 is titled the Cultural Encapsulation Level and includes counseling programs where multicultural issues are all but ignored and not seen as relevant to counseling training (Stage 1: Culturally Entrenched Stage) or are dealt with minimally through the acknowledgment that traditional models of counseling may not apply equally well to culturally diverse groups (Stage 2: Cross-Cultural Awakening Stage). Level 2 is termed the Conscientious Level of Counselor Education and includes programs that acknowledge the role of culture in counseling and have added a focused course on multicultural issues (Stage 3: Cultural Integrity Stage), or programs that go beyond a single course and infuse multicultural issues throughout the whole training philosophy and curriculum (Stage 4: Infusion Stage). In linking the D'Andrea and Daniels (1991) and Copeland (1982) models, Stage 3 most closely parallels Copeland's (1982) separate course model, and Stage 4 parallels Copeland's integration model.

D'Andrea and Daniels (1991) are of the view that the majority of counseling programs operate out of Stage 2 (the Cross-Cultural Awakening Stage), although there appears to be effort among some programs to move into Stage 3 (the Cultural Integrity Stage). The information used to develop D'Andrea and Daniels's (1991) developmental framework was generated primarily from informal contacts of the authors (e.g., discussion with colleagues and students from various programs) and a review of the journal literature.

A systematic national survey of counseling psychology programs yielded fruitful information regarding current multicultural training implementation methods. Hills and Strozier (1992) surveyed 49 APA-approved counseling psychology programs regarding multicultural coursework, faculty involvement in multicultural activities, minority student representation, and pressures experienced by programs to address multicultural issues. With regard to the coursework variable, survey results indicated that 87% of the programs offered at least one multicultural course, and 59% of programs required at least one such course of all students. Furthermore, in 63% of the programs multicultural units were offered in from 1 to 13 other courses. Five responding programs noted that it was a matter of departmental policy that all courses include coverage of multicultural issues. Finally, in 45% of the programs, students could develop a multicultural specialty through related coursework and practicums.

For those supportive of multicultural education in counseling training, the results of the Hills and Strozier (1992) survey are encouraging. It appears that counseling training programs are by and large developing and including a multicultural course in the curriculum and a smaller percentage are attempting to either infuse multiculturalism throughout the whole training philosophy or develop specialties in the area for interested students. A good percentage of the responding APA-approved programs would fit into D'Andrea and Daniels's (1991) more advanced Stage 4; and it appears that all methods described by Copeland (1982) over a decade ago are still indeed in use today.

It is important to note that early surveys and writings tended to focus on curriculum (courses) and that moving to a multicultural institution in counseling and clinical programs requires the implementation of multicultural organizational principles (see Chapter 4 for characteristics). Especially helpful for assessing the stage of multicultural institutional development and for suggesting potential strategies and goals are two instruments: the Multicultural Competency Checklist (Ponterotto, Alexander,

& Grieger, 1995) and the Multicultural Environment Inventory (Pope-Davis & Lui, 1996). Both are based on the assumption that the total system (not just coursework) must be addressed. For example, the Multicultural Competency Checklist addresses six potential areas within a training program: Minority Representation, Curriculum Issues, Counseling Practice and Supervision, Research Considerations, Student and Faculty Competency Evaluation, and Physical Environment. The domains of the Multicultural Environment Inventory include Evaluation/Assessment, Curriculum, Environment, Procedural Mechanisms, Global Attitudes, Research and Mentoring/Support.

Multicultural Organizational Assessment: A Case Example

The following is an example of an analysis of a graduate training program in counseling/clinical psychology with respect to their desire to become a more multicultural institution. This report, with changes to protect confidentiality, was sent to all faculty and staff of a major training institution after an extensive analysis. It exemplifies the basic principles and philosophy of multicultural organizational change.

To: Administration, Faculty, Staff, and Students
From: Multicultural Organizational Consultant
Re: Moving to a Multicultural Institution

After an extensive evaluation of your program, I have become increasingly aware of the many conflicts and issues related to making your institution more multicultural. Having worked in the field for more than 25 years, I have had the opportunity to observe the major obstacles to implementing diversity/multicultural initiatives in many organizations, and the methods/conditions that have proven most effective in overcoming them. As I view your department from a systemic vantage point, it is clear to me that change must be organizational in nature rather than in isolated subsystems of the program. It is with this thought in mind that I suggest the following plan for faculty/staff/student consideration. Please note that some of these suggestions may already be operational in some form or another. Also, they are given in a skeleton outline and need to be fleshed out more fully.

Multicultural Competencies Evaluation Plan for the
Graduate School of Counseling/Clinical Psychology

I would like to propose that your program support a broad evaluation plan to ascertain the school's multicultural development as it pertains to seven areas: (a) faculty and student competency evaluation; (b) curriculum issues; (c) minority representation; (d) therapeutic practice and supervision; (e) research considerations; (f) support services; and (g) programs, policies, and practices. Such a comprehensive evaluation would serve several purposes. First, it would help guide the school in its efforts to address multicultural issues. Research on multicultural organizational development recognizes that all institutions vary along a continuum of monocultural to multicultural characteristics, and that maximum and effective change occurs through a systemic intervention plan rather than compartmentalized changes addressing isolated subsystems. Second, such a comprehensive assessment would provide valuable data as to how well your program is doing in the education and training of future professional psychologists with multicultural expertise. Especially noteworthy has been the recent endorsements by several divisions of the American Psychological Association and the American Counseling Association of multicultural therapeutic competencies. Indeed, your school has also developed its own internal multicultural standards for both students and faculty but they need to be operationalized. Third, embarking on such an important venture may produce data on multicultural training with important implications to other training institutions and the wider psychological community. I envision the possibility of accumulating a large body of data related to a number of researchable questions with relevance to the education and training of multiculturally competent psychologists.

This proposal is still in its infancy, so I welcome feedback from all faculty, staff, and students. In general, the plan is (a) to systematically assess the multicultural competency of students from the time they enter your program until they graduate; (b) to assess and encourage faculty in multicultural development; (c) to analyze and make suggestions regarding the infusion of multicultural content into course work; (d) to analyze, develop, and monitor the development of practicum and internships with respect to multiculturalism; and (e) to conduct an institutional audit of the school's policies, practices, and structures to ascertain whether they enhance or negate movement toward becoming a multicultural organization. It is believed that such a formal undertaking would be a "first" in any psychology training program and could serve as a model protocol for the type of institutional change required to become multicultural.

Goal 1: Assessing Student Multicultural Competence

Your graduate program has committed itself to developing multi-culturally competent psychologists through the education and train-ing process. Other than requiring students to take and pass several courses in multicultural psychology, no overall long-term evaluation plan has been implemented to assess the development of multi-cultural competence among students. I propose an evaluation mecha-nism that would measure the degree of multicultural awareness, knowledge, and skills students possess (a) prior to their educational training, (b) periodically throughout their tenure at your school, and (c) on receipt of their doctoral degrees. Not only would such a project allow us to carefully monitor the effectiveness of multicultural train-ing, but the potential research contributions to the profession at large may be quite significant. At the present time, I propose that all entering students in the fall of next year be asked to participate in a longitudinal study of their multicultural counseling/therapy develop-ment. Prior to the beginning of course work, and two other times during their graduate work, they would be asked to fill out measures of multicultural counseling competence, measures of racial/cultural identity development, social attitudinal measures of multi-culturalism, and a demographic questionnaire. In addition, qualita-tive measures will be developed and used to assess the subjective experiences of multicultural training for selected students in the program. It may be helpful to identify a research team or group that would take responsibility for the research implementation and analy-sis. Because this is an exciting and important venture, I envision that a number of students interested in completing their doctoral disser-tations might be enlisted to participate in this portion of the evalu-ation plan. Some sample measures to consider include the following:

1. Multicultural Counseling Inventory (Sodowsky, Taffe, Gutkin, & Wise, 1994)
2. Multicultural Awareness-Knowledge-Skills Survey (D'Andrea, Daniels, & Heck, 1991)
3. Multicultural Counseling Awareness Scale (Ponterotto, Sanchez, & Magids, 1991)

4. Cross-Cultural Counseling Inventory-R (LaFromboise, Coleman, & Hernandez, 1991)
5. Counselor Effectiveness Rating Scale (Atkinson & Caskaddon, 1975)

Goal 2: Assessing Faculty Multicultural Competence

It is my contention that all theories of counseling and psychotherapy are culture specific and that multiculturalism is a fourth dimension that inevitably affects all aspects of psychology. Multicultural competence of faculty is, therefore, a necessity and must be manifest in teaching, curriculum, research, and supervision. I recognize that we are all victims of our cultural conditioning and education. As such, we are likely to be more conversant with Euro-American concepts and theories and may unintentionally restrict or block the educational opportunities of students to integrate the concepts of multiculturalism into their learning. Two aspects of multiculturalism are related to faculty development. First, learning opportunities such as how to include multicultural content into class material, how to facilitate difficult dialogues in the classroom, and how to become increasingly multicultural in outlook and practice are important. Second, formal means of assessing and monitoring the development of multicultural competence in the faculty need to be developed. Some ideas related to this later goal include the following:

1. All instructor evaluation forms should contain questions directly related to (a) how well the instructor has integrated multiculturalism into the content of the course, (b) how well they were able to facilitate multicultural discussions in class, and (c) their overall awareness, knowledge, and skills on the topic. In addition, some mechanism should be developed that allows for the specific assessment of multicultural competence by students of color. The evaluation of faculty by all students is valuable; however, I believe that students of color may have different or more meaningful observations of both the instructor and the course content. Although these forms may be used for promotion and tenure decisions, they are not meant to be punitive, but to provide feedback to instructors as to their strengths and limitations in infusing multiculturalism into course work.
2. A systematic study of all course syllabi on racial/ethnic/cultural minority themes should be undertaken. I propose that such a study should cover a 5-year period to ascertain how faculty have handled this requirement. Courses could be grouped into categories (research, assessment, intervention, and so forth) and analyzed for how such a

requirement is being met. What readings are being used? Is the topic covered in lectures and specific class activities? Is multiculturalism an ancillary topic in the course or infused throughout? What lessons or recommendations might arise from such a study? This is a project that could be undertaken in a master's thesis or doctoral dissertation.

3. I would also suggest that the faculty affairs committee and the curriculum committee begin to develop, infuse, monitor, and evaluate faculty on multicultural competencies.

Goal 3: Curriculum Development

Four major approaches or methods for integrating multicultural contents into psychology programs have been advocated: the separate course model, the area of concentration model, the interdisciplinary model, and the integration model. The separate course model involves adding a multicultural course to the existing curriculum. Extending the single-course approach, the area of concentration model includes a core of courses that usually include skill-building activities and practicums. The interdisciplinary model involves taking cultural-focused courses outside one's program in such disciplines as anthropology, sociology, economics, and ethnic studies. This model provides for a broadened theoretical base with regard to multicultural issues. Finally, the integration model involves infusing multicultural issues into all courses and training experiences. Currently, I believe your program operates from both the separate course and area of concentration models. Although these approaches have advantages, their disadvantages are that multicultural competence (a) cannot be achieved through a single course, (b) a specialization area does not reach all students, and (c) multiculturalism continues to be seen as an adjunct or in isolation from the broader curriculum. Thus, the only viable approach that transcends these problems is the integration model. Several suggestions may be made.

1. Faculty monitoring and evaluation for multicultural competence and a systematic evaluation of course syllabi as previously suggested would aid in this endeavor.

2. The formation of faculty working committees divided along course content for specific classes (theory, research, practice, assessment, and so on) would be charged with working on protocols (readings, content, activities, resources, and so on), which infuse multiculturalism into the classes and experiences of students. For example, the principles of psychotherapy class would have a specific protocol of multicultural infusion that would allow instructors to use as a guide.

3. I also advocate the formation of forums or focus groups that would involve students (especially students of color) in providing feedback about their experiences in classes with respect to multicultural adequacy, identifying the types of barriers they encounter in class, and eliciting suggestions of how to make the classroom experience more multiculturally meaningful.

4. Many other institutions have also wrestled with integrating multicultural content into regular course work. Compiling data and information on what they have done might prove valuable because we save time by not "reinventing the wheel" and can consider other protocols of multicultural infusion. Again, this may be a worthy dissertation topic that might prove of interest to one of your students.

5. Comprehensive examinations in all areas must contain multicultural content/issues/questions. Special committees can be charged with this task and reevaluate current exam content/format.

Goal 4: Minority Representation

Moving to a multicultural educational institution is helped immensely by the diversity present in the organization. Diversity should be encouraged in the student population, staff, faculty, and administration. Statistics regarding racial/ethnic minority representation should be constantly updated and your school should attempt to achieve some representational standard as a measure of multicultural commitment.

1. Admissions criteria should recognize multicultural competence and expertise as highly desirable. The admissions committee should continue to monitor the use of culturally appropriate standards for students applying to the School.

2. Hiring of faculty (core and adjunct) and staff should also value multicultural expertise.

Goal 5: Therapeutic Practice and Supervision

Becoming multiculturally competent in practice depends not only on coursework, but on actual experiences related to working with a culturally diverse population. Thus, making sure that students are specifically evaluated for their multicultural clinical proficiency, receive supervision from multiculturally competent supervisors, and obtain practicums and internships that provide work with a culturally diverse population are essential.

1. It is imperative that multicultural clinical proficiency be demonstrated in the exams and that a multicultural analysis of all cases should be required. Specific questions addressing multicultural issue must become a standard part of any clinical oral and written examination.
2. It is recommended that all practicum and internship sites be evaluated for the adequacy of multicultural training that they provide (supervision, diverse population, and so on).
3. All practicum or intern evaluations should contain a strong multicultural component. Likewise, all evaluations of clinical supervisors should also address their multicultural competence. Examples of such rating scales can be found in a number of publications.

Goal 6: Research

The faculty research committee has developed research competencies with importance placed on multiculturalism. Again, these competencies need to be operationalized into the entire training program. Although a number of faculty have active research programs dealing with racial/ethnic, gender, and sexual orientation issues, there is a strong need to ensure that multicultural issues are appropriately covered in research, proposal design, and dissertation-related courses. It is critical that multicultural issues are considered in the conceptualization and design of research to allow for generalizability of research results to similar populations of individuals. Furthermore, such emphasis would allow students to engage in the process of "deconstruction" so that even when they are researching a primarily Euro-American population using a logical positivist approach, they are able to discuss or unmask the cultural assumptions inherent in their study.

1. The faculty research committee should develop, implement, and monitor the operationalization of multicultural research competencies in course work and dissertations. The committee might consider requiring all students to briefly discuss the multicultural assumptions, limitations, and issues in their dissertations.
2. All dissertation chairs and committee members should make a concerted effort to guide students in understanding the multicultural issues inherent in their proposed study.
3. Instructors of specific research courses would be asked to not only cover the multicultural research competencies, but introduce students to a diversity of research methods (modern/postmodern and qualitative/quantitative). At the present time, most multicultural research tends to be postmodern in orientation.

Goal 7: Support Services

The campus or school climate is often an invalidating experience for students of color. Thus, as your school begins to develop into a more multicultural environment, support services sensitive to the "minority experience" are crucial to maximize learning and increase retention and graduation rates for students of color. A multicultural affairs committee or some other internal mechanism empowered to supply leadership and support to the school's program is needed. The office of the director of multicultural affairs and student/faculty minority group organizations (formal and informal) seem well positioned to play these crucial roles.

Goal 8: Institutional Audit of Programs, Policies, and Practices

Multicultural organizational development (MOD) is a relatively new term, originally used in a business setting to facilitate using the full potential of a diverse workforce. All organizations whether business or industry, government, mental health agency, or educational institution have an organizational culture. These patterns are communicated to new members as the appropriate ways to perceive, think, and feel in relation to its problems. MOD attempts to change, refine, instill, or create new policies, programs, practices, and structures that are multicultural thus moving the organization from a monocultural to a multicultural entity becomes the objective.

Understanding how the organizational and institutional culture at your school enhances or negates the development of multicultural competence is crucial to productive development. In other words, it does little good that individual instructors may present multicultural content to students when the very organization that employs them is filled with monocultural policies and practices. In many cases, organizational customs do not value or allow the use of cultural knowledge or skills in the educational context. Educational institutions may even actively discourage, negate, or punish multicultural expressions among its faculty and students. Thus, it is imperative to view multicultural competence for organizations as well. Developing new rules, regulations, policies, practices, and structures that enhance multiculturalism are important and requires an institutional audit. I recognize that this last task may prove the most difficult to implement. Multicultural organizational development, however, is a long-term process that requires considerable commitment from your program.

1. A multicultural audit of the school's programs, policies, and practices can best be accomplished using some form of assessment tool. Several are available for us to use, modify, or both.

2. A systemic analysis of the graduate program needs to be undertaken. Your divisional area structure; formation, charge, and composition of faculty committees; advising/admissions systems; policies related to the hiring, retention, and promotion of faculty; staff/faculty, student/faculty, faculty/administration, relations, and so forth; and many other aspects of the school need to be reexamined.

3. I suggest the development of a mechanism or process by which such an assessment might be accomplished (internal committee or outside consultant). This group or committee would be empowered to recommend and implement new policy. Its task would not only be to conduct an audit, but to oversee the strategic action plan associated with multicultural development.

Please note that this proposal is a working one and that many of you may have alternative suggestions for making your program a more multiculturally oriented institution. I recognize the incompleteness of my ideas and realize that this proposal is ambitious, requires immense time and resources, and is long-term in nature. If, however, we value multiculturalism as we profess to do, your school must take the road less traveled.

Conclusion

It is clear that becoming multiculturally competent at the personal, professional, and organizational level is not an easy task. We can no longer afford to treat multiculturalism as an ancillary, rather than an integral part of mental health practice. The viability and relevance of our profession, and indeed our society, depends on how we meet the challenge of multiculturalism. If we truly believe that multiculturalism is intrinsic and crucial for our nation, then ethnocentric monoculturalism should be seen as unhealthy in a pluralistic society.

References

Adler, N. J. (1986). Cultural synergy: Managing the impact of cultural diversity. In *1986 annual: Developing human resources*. San Diego, CA: University Associates.

Alba, R. D. (1990). *Ethnic identity: The transformation of White America*. New Haven, CT: Yale University Press.

Albert, R. D. (1983). The intercultural sensitizer or culture assimilator: A cognitive approach. In D. Landis & R. W. Brislin (Eds.), *Handbook of intercultural training: Vol. 2. Issues in training methodology* (pp. 86-217). New York: Pergamon.

Alexander, C. M., & Sussman, L. (1995). Creative approaches to multicultural counseling. In J. G. Ponterotto, J. M. Casas, L. A. Suzuki, & C. M. Alexander (Eds.), *Handbook of multicultural counseling* (pp. 375-384). Thousand Oaks, CA: Sage.

Alvarez, A., Batson, R. M., Carr, A. K., Parks, P., Peck, H. B., Shervington, W., Tyler, R. B., & Zwerling, I. (1976). *Racism, elitism, professionalism: Barriers to community mental health*. New York: Jason Aronson.

American Counseling Association. (1995). *Code of ethics and standards of practice*. Alexandria, VA: Author.

American Psychological Association. (1986). *Accreditation handbook*. Washington, DC: Author.

American Psychological Association. (1992). *Ethical principles of psychologists and code of conduct*. Washington, DC: Author.

American Psychological Association. (1993). Guidelines for providers of psychological services to ethnic, linguistic, and culturally diverse populations. *American Psychologist, 48*, 45-48.

Arredondo, P., Toporek, R., Brown, S. P., Jones, J., Locke, D. C., Sanchez, J., & Stadler, H. (1996). Operationalization of the multicultural counseling competencies. *Journal of Multicultural Counseling and Development, 24*, 42-78.

Asante, M. (1987). *The Afrocentric idea*. Philadelphia, PA: Temple University Press.

Atkinson, D. R., & Caskaddon, G. (1975). A prestigious introduction, psychological jargon, and perceived counselor credibility. *Journal of Counseling Psychology, 22,* 180-186.

Atkinson, D. R., & Lowe, S. M. (1995). The role of ethnicity, cultural knowledge, and conventional techniques in counseling and psychotherapy. In J. G. Ponterotto, J. M. Casas, L. A. Suzuki, & C. M. Alexander (Eds.), *Handbook of multicultural counseling* (pp. 387-414). Thousand Oaks, CA: Sage.

Atkinson, D. R., Maruyama, M., & Matsui, S. (1978). The effects of counselor race and counseling approach on Asian Americans' perceptions of counselor credibility and utility. *Journal of Counseling Psychology, 25,* 76-83.

Atkinson, D. R., Morten, G., & Sue, D. W. (1993). *Counseling American minorities*. Dubuque, IA: Brown & Benchmark.

Atkinson, D. R., Morten, G., & Sue, D. W. (1998). *Counseling American minorities* (5th ed.). Boston: McGraw-Hill.

Atkinson, D. R., Thompson, C. E., & Grant, S. K. (1993). A three-dimensional model for counseling racial/ethnic minorities. *Counseling Psychologist, 21,* 257-277.

Baldwin, J. A., & Bell, Y. R. (1985). The African Self-Consciousness Scale: An Africentric personality questionnaire. *Western Journal of Black Studies, 9,* 61-68.

Barongan, C., Bernal, G., Comas-Diaz, L., Iijima Hall, C. C., Nagayama Hall, G. C., LaDue, R. A., Parham, T. A., Pedersen, P. B., Porche-Burke, L. M., Rollock, D., & Root, M. P .P. (1997). Misunderstandings of multiculturalism: Shouting fire in crowded theaters. *American Psychologist, 52,* 654-655.

Barr, D. J., & Strong, L. J. (1987, May). Embracing multiculturalism: The existing contradictions. *ACU-I Bulletin,* pp. 20-23.

Bennett, M. J. (1986). A developmental approach to training for intercultural sensitivity. *International Journal of Intercultural Relations, 10,* 179-196.

Bernal, M. E., & Knight, G. P. (1993). *Ethnic idenity: Formation and transmission among Hispanics and other minorities*. Albany: State University of New York Press.

Betancourt, H., & Lopez, S. R. (1993). The study of culture, ethnicity, and race in American psychology. *American Psychologist, 48,* 629-637.

Brislin, R. W., Cushner, K., Cherri, C., & Young, M. (1986). *Intercultural interactions: A practical guide*. Newbury Park, CA: Sage.

Brown, D. (1996). Reply to Derald Wing Sue. *Spectrum, 57*(2), 5-7.

California Association of Social Rehabilitation Agencies. (1985). *Standards for social rehabilitation services*. Emeryville, CA: Author.

Carcuff, R. R., & Anthony, W. A. (1979). *The skills of helping*. Amherst, MA: Human Resource Development Press.

Carney, C. G., & Kahn, K. B. (1984). Building competencies for effective cross-cultural counseling: A developmental view. *Counseling Psychologist, 12*(1), 11-119.

Carter, R. T. (1990). The relationship between racism and racial identity among White Americans: An exploratory investigation. *Journal of Counseling and Development, 69,* 46-50.

Carter, R. T. (1995). *The influence of race and racial identity in psychotherapy*. New York: John Wiley.

Casas, J. M., & Pytluk, S. D. (1995). Hispanic identity development. In J. G. Ponterotto, J. M. Casas, L. A. Suzuki, & C. M. Alexander (Eds.) *Handbook of multicultural counseling* (pp. 155-180). Thousand Oaks, CA: Sage.

Cheatham, H. E. (1994). A response. *Counseling Psychologist, 22,* 290-295.

Choney, S. K., Berryhill-Paapke, E., & Robbins, R. R. (1995). The acculturation of American Indians: Developing frameworks for research and practice. In J. G. Ponterotto, J. M. Casas, L. A. Suzuki, & C. M. Alexander (Eds.), *Handbook of multicultural counseling* (pp. 73-92). Thousand Oaks, CA: Sage.

Christopher, J. C. (1996). Counseling's inescapable moral visions. *Journal of Counseling and Development, 75*, 17-25.

Cook, D. A., & Helms, J. E. (1988). Visible racial/ethnic group supervisees' satisfaction with cross-cultural supervision as predicted by relationship characteristics. *Journal of Counseling Psychology, 35*, 268-274.

Copeland, E. J. (1982). Minority populations and traditional counseling programs: Some alternatives. *Counselor Education and Supervision, 21*, 187-193.

Copeland, L. (1988, May). Learning to manage a multicultural workforce. *Training*, pp. 49-56.

Cross, T. L. (1995/1996). Developing a knowledge base to support cultural competence. *Family Resource Coalition Report, 14*, 3-4.

Cross, T. L., Bazron, B. J., Dennis, K. W., & Isaacs, M. R. (1989). *Toward a culturally competent system of care.* Washington, DC: Child and Adolescent Service System Program Technical Assistance Center.

Cross, W. E. (1971). The Negro-to-Black conversion experience: Toward a psychology of Black liberation. *Black World, 20*, 13-27.

Cross, W. E. (1978). The Cross and Thomas models of psychological nigrescence. *Journal of Black Psychology, 5*, 13-19.

Cross, W. E. (1989). Nigrescence: A nondiaphanous phenomena. *Counseling Psychologist, 17*, 273-276.

Cross, W. E. (1991). *Shades of Black: Diversity in African American identity.* Philadelphia, PA: Temple University Press.

Cross, W. E. (1995). The psychology of Nigrescence: Revising the Cross model. In J. G. Ponterotto, J. M. Casas, L. A. Suzuki, & C. M. Alexander (Eds.), *Handbook of multicultural counseling* (pp. 93-122). Thousand Oaks, CA: Sage.

Cross, W. E., Parham, T. A., & Helms, J. E. (1991). Nigrescence revisited: Theory and research. In R. L. Jones (Ed.), *Advances in black psychology* (pp. 319-338). Los Angeles: Cobb & Henry.

D'Andrea, M., & Daniels, J. (1991). Exploring the different levels of multicultural counseling training in counselor education. *Journal of Counseling and Development, 70*, 78-85.

D'Andrea, M., Daniels, J., & Heck, R. (1991). Evaluating the impact of multicultural counseling training. *Journal of Counseling and Development, 70*, 143-150.

Das, A. K. (1987). Indigenous models of therapy in traditional Asian societies. *Journal of Multicultural Counseling and Development, 15*, 25-37.

Dauphinais, R., Dauphinais, L., & Rowe, W. (1981). Effects of race and communication style on Indian perceptions of counselor effectiveness. *Counselor Education and Supervision, 21*, 72-80.

Downing, N. E., & Roush, K. L. (1985). From passive acceptance to active commitment: A model of feminist identity development for women. *Counseling Psychologist, 13*, 695-709.

Egan, G. (1982). *The skilled helper* (2nd ed.). Monterey, CA: Brooks/Cole.

Ethnic Populations Services Planning Task Force. (1988). *Ethnic populations mental health services in Santa Clara county: A long-term solution to community distress.* San Jose, CA: Santa Clara County Health Department.

Feagin, J. R. (1989). *Racial & ethnic relations.* Englewood Cliffs, NJ: Prentice Hall.

Foster, B. G., Jackson, G., Cross, W. E., Jackson, B., & Hardiman, R. (1988). Workforce diversity and business (Reprint from *Training and Development Journal,* April 1988). Alexandria, VA: American Society for Training and Development.

Fowers, B. J., & Richardson, F. C. (1996). Why is multiculturalism good? *American Psychologist, 51,* 609-621.

Fukuyama, M. A. (1990). Taking a universal approach to multicultural counseling. *Counselor Education and Supervision, 30,* 6-17.

Gallegos, J. S. (1982). Planning and administering services for minority groups. In M. J. Austin & W. E. Hershey (Eds.), *Handbook on mental health adminstration* (pp. 87-105). San Francisco: Jossey-Bass.

Gergen, K. J. (1994). Exploring the postmodern: Perils or potentials? *American Psychologist, 49,* 412-416.

Golden, M. (1992, May 13). Taking over the asylum. *Bay Guardian,* p. 12.

Gonzalez, R. C. (1997). Postmodern supervision: A multicultural perspective. In D. B. Pope-Davis & H. L. K. Coleman (Eds.), *Multicultural counseling competencies: Assessment, education and training, and supervision* (pp. 350-386). Thousand Oaks, CA: Sage.

Gordon, M. M. (1964). *Assimilation in American life.* New York: Oxford University Press.

Grier, W., & Cobbs, P. (1968). *Black rage.* New York: Basic Books.

Grier, W., & Cobbs, P. (1971). *The Jesus bag.* San Francisco: McGraw-Hill.

Gunnings, T., & Simpkins, G. (1972). A systemic approach to counseling disadvantaged youth. *Personnel and Guidance Journal, 50,* 29-35.

Guthrie, R. V. (1976). *Even the rat was White.* New York: Harper & Row.

Hall, W. S., Cross, W. E., & Freedle, R. (1972). Stages in the development of Black awareness: An exploratory investigation. In R. L. Jones (Ed.), *Black psychology* (pp. 156-165). New York: Harper & Row.

Halleck, S. L. (1971, April). Therapy is the handmaiden of the status quo. *Psychology Today, 4,* 30-34, 98-100.

Hammerschlag, C. A. (1988). *The dancing healers.* San Francisco: Harper & Row.

Hardiman, R. (1982). White identity development: A process-oriented model for describing the racial consciousess of White Americans. *Dissertation Abstracts International, 43,* 104A. (University Microfilms No. 82-10330)

Harner, M. (1990). *The way of the shaman.* San Francisco: Harper & Row.

Heinrich, R. K., Corbin, J. L., & Thomas, K. R. (1990). Counseling Native Americans. *Journal of Counseling and Development, 69,* 128-133.

Helms, J. E. (1984). Toward a theoretical model of the effects of race on counseling: A Black and White model. *Counseling Psychologist, 12,* 153-165.

Helms, J. E. (1986). Expanding racial identity theory to cover counseling process. *Journal of Counseling Psychology, 33,* 62-64.

Helms, J. E. (1990). *Black and White racial identity: Theory, research, and practice.* New York: Greenwood.

Helms, J. E. (1994a). How multiculturalism obscures racial factors in the therapy process: Comment on Ridley et al. (1994), Sodowsky et al. (1994), Ottavi et al. (1994), and Thompson et al. (1994). *Journal of Counseling Psychology, 41,* 162-165.

Helms, J. E. (1994b). Racial identity and other "racial" constructs. In E. J. Trickett, R. J. Watts, & D. Birman (Eds.), *Human diversity* (pp. 285-311). San Francisco: Jossey-Bass.

Helms, J. E. (1995). An update of Helms's White and people of color racial identity models. In J. G. Ponterotto, J. M. Casas, L. A. Suzuki, & C. M. Alexander (Eds.), *Handbook of multicultural counseling* (pp. 181-191). Thousand Oaks, CA: Sage.

Helms, J. E., & Richardson, T. Q. (1997). How "Multiculturalism" obscures race and culture as differential aspects of counseling competency. In D. B. Pope-Davis & H. L. K. Coleman (Eds.), *Multicultural counseling competencies: Assessment, education and training, and supervision* (pp. 60-79). Thousand Oaks, CA: Sage.

Highlen, P. S. (1994). Racial/ethnic diversity in doctoral programs of psychology: Challenges for the 21st century. *Applied & Preventive Psychology, 3,* 91-108.

Highlen, P. S. (1996). MCT theory and implications for organizations/systems. In D. W. Sue, A. E. Ivey, & P. B. Pedersen (Eds.), *A theory of multicultural counseling and therapy* (pp. 65-85). Pacific Grove, CA: Brooks/Cole.

Hills, H. I., & Strozier, A. A. (1992). Multicultural training in APA-approved counseling psychology programs: A survey. *Professional Psychology: Research and Practice, 23,* 43-51.

Hines, P. M., & Boyd-Franklin, N. (1996). African American families. In M. McGoldrick, J. Giordano, & J. K. Pearce (Eds.), *Ethnicity and family therapy* (pp. 66-84). New York: Guilford.

Hoshmand, L. S. T. (1989). Alternate research paradigms: A review and teaching proposal. *Counseling Psychologist, 17,* 3-79.

Ibrahim, F. A. (1985). Effective cross-cultural counseling and psychotherapy: A framework. *Counseling Psychologist, 13,* 625-638.

Ibrahim, F. A. (1991). Contribution of cultural worldview to generic counseling and development. *Journal of Counseling and Development, 70,* 13-19.

Isaac, R. J., & Armat, V. C. (1990). *Madness in the streets: How psychiatry and the law abandoned the mentally ill.* New York: Macmillan.

Ivey, A., & Authier, J. (1978). Microcounseling: Innovations in interview training. Springfield, IL: Charles C Thomas.

Ivey, A. E. (1981). Counseling and psychotherapy: Toward a new perspective. In A. J. Marsella & P. B. Pedersen (Eds.), *Cross-cultural counseling and psychotherapy* (pp. 173-193). New York: Pergamon.

Ivey, A. E. (1986). *Developmental therapy.* San Francisco: Jossey-Bass.

Ivey, A. E., Ivey, M. B., & Simek-Morgan, L. (1993). *Counseling and psychotherapy: A multicultural perspective.* Boston: Allyn & Bacon.

Jackson, B. (1975). Black identity development. *Journal of Educational Diversity, 2,* 19-25.

Jackson, M. L. (1995). Multicultural counseling: Historical perspectives. In J. G. Ponterotto, J. M. Casas, L. A. Suzuki, & C. M. Alexander (Eds.), *Handbook of multicultural counseling* (pp. 3-16). Thousand Oaks, CA: Sage.

Jaffee, B. (1982). Assessing community mental health needs. In M. J. Austin & W. E. Hershey (Eds.), *Handbook on mental health administration* (pp. 376-396). San Francsico: Jossey-Bass.

Jensen, M. (1992). *Multicultural organizational competencies.* Unpublished master's thesis, California State University, Hayward.

Jones, J. M. (1972). *Prejudice and racism.* Reading, MA: Addison Wesley.

Jones, J. M. (1997). *Prejudice and racism* (2nd ed.). New York: McGraw Hill.

Katz, J. (1985). The sociopolitical nature of counseling. *Counseling Psychologist, 13,* 615-624.

Katz, J., & Ivey, A. (1977). White awareness: The frontier of racism awareness training. *Personnel and Guidance Journal, 55,* 485-489.

Kerwin, C., & Ponterotto, J. G. (1995). Biracial idenity development: Theory and research. In J. G. Ponterotto, J. M. Casas, L. A. Suzuki, & C. M. Alexander (Eds.), *Handbook of multicultural counseling* (pp. 199-217). Thousand Oaks, CA: Sage.

Kim, J. (1981). The process of Asian American identity development: A study of Japanese American women's perceptions of their struggle to achieve personal identities as Americans of Asian ancestry. *Dissertation Abstracts International, 42,* 1551A. (University Microfilm No. 81-18080)

Kitano, H. L. (1982). Mental health in the Japanese American community. In E. E. Jones & S. J. Korchin (Eds.), *Minority mental health* (pp. 149-164). New York: Praeger.

Kluckhohn, F. R., & Strodtbeck, F. L. (1961). *Variations in value orientations.* Evanton, IL: Row, Paytterson, & Co.

Korman, M. (1974). National conference on levels and patterns of professional training in psychology: Major themes. *American Psychologist, 29,* 301-313.

Krogman, W. M. (1945). The concept of race. In R. Linton (Ed.), *The science of man in the world crisis* (pp. 38-62). New York: Columbia University Press.

LaFromboise, T. D., Coleman, H. L. K., & Hernandez, A. (1991). Development and factor structure of the Cross-Cultural Counseling Inventory-Revised. *Professional Psychology: Research and Practice, 22,* 380-388.

Laird, J., & Green, R. (1996). *Lesbians and gays in couples and families.* San Francisco: Jossey Bass.

Lee, C. C., & Armstrong, K. L. (1995). Indigenous models of mental health intervention: Lessons from traditional healers. In J. G. Ponterotto, J. M. Casas, L. A. Suzuki, & C. M. Alexander (Eds.), *Handbook of multicultural counseling* (pp. 441-456). Thousand Oaks, CA: Sage.

Lee, C. C., Oh, M. Y., & Mountcastle, A. R. (1992). Indigenous models of helping in nonwestern countries: Implications for multicultural counseling. *Journal of Multicultural Counseling and Development, 20,* 1-10.

Lee, F. Y. (1991). *The relationship of ethnic idenity to social support, self-esteem, psychological distress, and help-seeking behavior among Asian American colege students.* Unpublished doctoral dissertation, University of Illinois, Urbana-Champaign.

Lefley, H. P. (1990). Rehabilitation in mental illness: Insights from other cultures. *Psychosocial Rehabilitation Journal, 14,* 1, 5-11.

Linton, R. (Ed.). (1945). *The science of man in the world crisis.* New York: Columbia University Press.

Locke, D. C. (1990). A not so provincial view of multicultural counseling. *Counselor Education and Supervision, 30,* 18-25.

Margolis, R. L., & Runtga, S. A. (1986). Training counselors for work with special populations: A second look. *Journal of Counseling and Development, 64,* 642-644.

McCarn, S. R., & Fassinger, R. E. (1996). Revisioning sexual minority identity formation: A new model of lesbian identity and its implications for counseling and research. *Counseling Psychologist, 24*(3), 508-534.

McDavis, R. J., & Parker, M. (1977). A course on counseling ethnic minorities: A model. *Counselor Education and Supervision, 17,* 146-149.

McIntosh, P. (1989, July/August). White privilege: Unpacking the invisible knapsack. *Peace and Freedom,* pp. 8-10.

McNamara, K., & Richard, K. M. (1989). Feminist identity development: Implications for feminist therapy with women. *Journal of Counseling and Development, 68,* 184-193.

Merta, R. J., Stringham, E. M., & Ponterotto, J. G. (1988). Simulating culture shock in counselor trainees: An experiential exercise for cross-cultural training. *Journal of Counseling and Development, 66,* 242-245.

Meyers, H., Echemedia, F., & Trimble, J. E. (1991). American Indians and the counseling process. In P. B. Pedersen (Ed.), *Handbook of cross-cultural counseling* (pp. 3-9). Westport, CT: Greenwood.

Milliones, J. (1980). Construction of a black consciousness measure: Psychotherapeutic implications. *Psychotherapy: Theory, Research, and Practice, 17,* 175-182.

Morrison, A. M., & Von Glinow, M. A. (1990). Women and minorities in management. *American Psychologist, 45*(2), 200-208.

Munoz, R. H., & Sanchez, A. M. (1996). *Developing culturally competent systems of care for state mental health services.* Boulder, CO: WICHE.

Nakao, A. (1990, March 23). Mental health system ill-equipped for racial minorities. *San Francisco Examiner,* p. A12.

Ness, C. (1992, February 2). Eurocentrism gains a voice. *San Francisco Examiner,* pp. B1, B4.

Nwachuku, U., & Ivey, A. (1991). Culture-specific counseling: An alternative approach. *Journal of Counseling and Development, 70,* 106-111.

Packer, A. H., & Johnston, W. B. (1987). *Workforce 2000: Work and workers for the 21st century.* Indianapolis, IN: Hudson Institute.

Paniagua, F. A. (1994). *Assessing and treating culturally diverse clients.* Thousand Oaks, CA: Sage.

Parham, T. A. (1989). Cycles of psychological nigrescence. *Counseling Psychologist, 17,* 187-226.

Parham, T. A. (1997). An African-centered view of dual relationships. In B. Herlihy & G. Corey (Eds.), *Boundary issues in counseling* (pp. 109-112). Alexandria, VA: American Counseling Association.

Parham, T. A., & Helms, J. E. (1981). The influence of Black students' racial attitutdes on preferences for counselor's race. *Journal of Counseling Psychology, 28,* 250-257.

Parker, M., & McDavis, R. J. (1979). An awareness experience: Toward counseling minorities. *Counselor Education and Supervision, 18,* 312-317.

Pedersen, P. (1988). *A handbook for developing multicultural awareness.* Alexandria, VA: American Association for Counseling and Development.

Pedersen, P. (1991a). Multiculturalism as a generic approach to counseling. *Journal of Counseling and Development, 70*(1), 6-12.

Pedersen, P. (1991b). Multiculturalism as a fourth force in counseling [Special issue]. *Journal of Counseling and Development, 70.*

Pedersen, P. (1994). *A handbook for developing multicultural awarenss* (2nd ed.). Alexandria, VA: American Counseling Association.

Pettigrew, T. F. (1988). Integration and pluralism. In P. Katz & D. A. Taylor (Eds.), *Eliminating racism: Profiles in controversy* (pp. 19-30). New York: Plenum.

Phinney, J. S., & Rotheram, M. J. (Eds.). (1987). *Children's ethnic socialization: Pluralism and development.* Newbury Park, CA: Sage.

Pinderhughes, E. (1989). *Understanding race, ethnicity, and power: The key to efficacy in clinical practice.* New York: Free Press.

Ponterotto, J. G. (1988). Racial/ethnic minority research in the *Journal of Counseling Psychology:* A content analysis and methodological critique. *Journal of Counseling Psychology, 53,* 410-418.

Ponterotto, J. G., Alexander, C. M., & Grieger, I. (1995). A multicultural counseling checklist for counseling training programs. *Journal of Multicultural Counseling and Development, 23,* 11-20.

Ponterotto, J. G., & Benesch, K. F. (1988). An organizational framework for understanding the role of culture in counseling. *Journal of Counseling and Development, 66,* 237-241.

Ponterotto, J. G., & Casas, J. M. (1991). *Handbook of racial/ethnic minority counseling research.* Springfield, IL: Charles C Thomas.

Ponterotto, J. G., Casas, J. M., Suzuki, L. A., & Alexander, C. M. (Eds.). (1995). *Handbook of multicultural counseling.* Thousand Oaks, CA: Sage.

Ponterotto, J. G., & Pedersen, P. B. (1993). *Preventing prejudice.* Newbury Park, CA: Sage.

Ponterotto, J. G., Rieger, B. P., Barrett, A., & Sparks, R. (1994). Assessing multicultural counseling competence: A review of instrumentation. *Journal of Counseling and Development, 72,* 316-322.

Ponterotto, J. G., & Sabnani, H. B. (1989). "Classics" in multicultural counseling: A systematic 5-year content analysis. *Journal of Multicultural Counseling and Development, 17,* 23-37.

Ponterotto, J. G., Sanchez, C. M., & Magids, D. M. (1991, August). *Initial development and validation of the Multicultural Counseling Awareness Scale.* Paper presented at the annual meeting of the American Psychological Association, San Francisco.

Ponterotto, J. G., & Wise, S. L. (1987). Construct validity of the Racial Identity Attitude Scale. *Journal of Counseling Psychology, 34,* 218-223.

Pope-Davis, D. B., & Coleman, H. L. K. (1997). *Multicultural counseling competencies: Assessment, education and training, and supervision.* Thousand Oaks, CA: Sage.

Pope-Davis, D. B., & Lui, W. (1995). *The multicultural environment inventory.* Unpublished manuscript, University of Maryland, College Park.

President's Commission on Mental Health. (1980). *Report from the President's Commission on Mental Health.* Washington, DC: Government Printing Office.

Ramirez, M., III. (1983). *Psychology of the Americas: Mestizo perspectives on personality and mental health.* New York: Pergamon.

Redmond, S. P. (1990). Mentoring and cultural diversity in academic settings. *American Behavioral Scientist, 34,* 188-200.

Ridley, C. R. (1984). Clinical treatment of the nondisclosing Black client. *American Psychologist, 39,* 1234-1244.

Ridley, C. R. (1995). *Overcoming unintentional racism in counseling and therapy: A practitioner's guide to intentional intervention.* Thousand Oaks, CA: Sage.

Ridley, C. R., Mendoza, D. W., Kanitz, B. E., Angermeier, L., & Zenk, R. (1994). Cultural sensitivity in multiucltural counseling: A perceptual schema model. *Journal of Counseling Psychology, 41*(2), 125-136.

Root, M. P. P. (1992). *Racially mixed people in America.* Newbury Park, CA: Sage.

Root, M. P. P. (1996). *The multiracial experience.* Thousand Oaks, CA: Sage.

Rowe, W., Behrens, J. T., & Leach, M. M. (1995). Racial/ethnic identity and racial consciousness: Looking back and looking forward. In J. G. Ponterotto, J. M. Casas, L. A. Suzuki, & C. M. Alexander (Eds.), *Handbook of multicultural counseling* (pp. 218-235). Thousand Oaks, CA: Sage.

Rowe, W., Bennett, S., & Atkinson, D. R. (1994). White racial identity models: A critique and alternative proposal. *Counseling Psychologist, 22,* 120-146.

Ruiz, A. S. (1990). Ethnic identity: Crisis and resolution. *Journal of Multicultural Counseling and Development, 18,* 29-40.

Ruiz, P., & Ruiz, P. P. (1983). Treatment compliance among Hispanics. *Journal of Operational Psychiatry, 14,* 112-114.

Ryan, R. A., & Ryan, L. (1989). *Multicultural aspects of chemical dependency treatment: An American Indian perspective.* Unpublished manuscript, Turnaround Adolescent Treatment Program, Vancover, WA.

Sabnani, H. B., & Ponterotto, J. G. (1992). Racial/ethnic minority instrumentation in counseling research: A review, critique, and recommendation. *Measurement and Evaluation in Counseling and Development, 24,* 161-187.

Sabnani, H. B., Ponterotto, J. G., & Borodovsky, L. G. (1991). White racial identity development and cross-cultural counselor training. *Counseling Psychologist, 19,* 76-102.

Schaefer, R. T. (1988). *Racial and ethnic groups* (3rd ed.). Glenview, IL: Scott Foresman.

Schein, E. H. (1990). Organizational culture. *American Psychologist, 45*(2), 109-119.

Sherover-Marcuse, R. (1994). Liberation theory: Axioms and working assumptions about the
perpetuation of social oppression. In N. G. Yuen (Ed.), *The politics of liberation* (pp. 1-
18). Dubuque, IA: Kendall/Hunt.

Smith, E. J. (1991). Ethnic identity development: Toward the development of a theory within
the context of majority/minority status. *Journal of Counseling and Development, 70,*
181-188.

Smith, E. J., & Vasquez, M. J. T. (1985). Introduction. *Counseling Psychologist, 13,* 531-536.

Snowden, L. R. & Cheung, F. K. (1990). Use of in-patient mental health services by members
of ethnic minority groups. *American Psychologist, 45,* 347-355.

Sodowsky, G. R., Taffe, R. C., Gutkin, T. B., & Wise, S. L. (1992). Development of the
Multicultural Counseling Inventory: A self-report measure of multicultural competencies.
Journal of Counseling Psychology, 41, 137-148.

Solomon, A. (1992). Clinical diagnosis among diverse populations: A multiucltural perspective. *Journal of Contemporary Human Services, June,* 371-377.

Spaniol, L., Zipple, A., & Cohen, B. (1991). Managing innovation and change in psychosocial
rehabilitation: Key principles and guidelines. *Psychosocial Rehabilitation Journal, 14*(3),
27-38.

Sue, D., Sue, D. W., & Sue, S. (1997). *Understanding abnormal behavior* (5th ed.). Boston:
Houghton-Mifflin.

Sue, D. W. (1977). Barriers to effective cross-culturlal counseling. *Journal of Counseling
Psychology, 24,* 420-429.

Sue, D. W. (1978). Eliminating cultural oppression in counseling: Toward a general theory.
Journal of Counseling Psychology, 25, 419-428.

Sue, D. W. (1981). *Counseling the culturally different: Theory and practice.* New York: John
Wiley.

Sue, D. W. (1990). Culture specific techniques in counseling: A conceptual framework.
Professional Psychology, 21, 424-433.

Sue, D. W. (1991a). A conceptual model for cultural diversity training. *Journal of Counseling
and Development, 70,* 99-105.

Sue, D. W. (1991b). A diversity perspective on contextualism. *Journal of Counseling and
Development, 70,* 300-301.

Sue, D. W. (1995a). Toward a theory of multicultural counseling and therapy. In J. A. Banks
& C. A. M. Banks (Eds.), *Handbook of research on multicultural education* (pp. 647-659).
New York: Macmillan.

Sue, D. W. (1995b). Multicultural organizational development: Implications for the counseling profession. In J. G. Ponterotto, J. M. Casas, L. A. Suzuki, & C. M. Alexander (Eds.),
Handbook of multicultural counseling (pp. 474-492). Thousand Oaks, CA: Sage.

Sue, D. W. (1996). ACES endorsement of the multicultural counseling competencies: Do we
have the courage. *Spectrum, 57*(1), 9-10.

Sue, D. W. (1997). Multiculturalism and discomfort. *Spectrum, 57*(3), 7-9.

Sue, D. W., Arredondo, P., & McDavis, R. J. (1992). Multicultural competencies/standards:
A pressing need. *Journal of Counseling and Development, 70*(4), 477-486.

Sue, D. W., Bernier, J. B., Durran, M., Feinberg, L., Pedersen, P., Smith, E., & Vasquez-Nut-
tall, E. (1982). Position paper: Cross-cultural counseling competencies. *Counseling Psychologist, 10,* 45-52.

Sue, D. W., & Frank, A. C. (1973). A topological approach to the study of Chinese- and Japanese American college males. *Journal of Social Issues, 29,* 129-148.

Sue, D. W., Ivey, A. E., & Pedersen, P. B. (1996). *A theory of multicultural counseling and therapy.* Pacific Grove, CA: Brooks/Cole.

Sue, D. W., & Sue, D. (1977). Barriers to effective cross-cultural counseling. *Journal of Counseling Psychology, 24,* 420-429.

Sue, D. W., & Sue, D. (1990). *Counseling the culturally different: Theory and practice.* New York: John Wiley.

Sue, S., McKinney, H., Allen, D., & Hall, J. (1975). Delivery of community mental health services to Black and White clients. *Journal of Consulting Psychology, 42,* 794-801.

Sue, S., & Sue, D. W. (1971). Chinese American personality and mental health. *Amerasian Journal, 1,* 36-49.

Sue, S., Ito, J., & Bradshaw, C. (1984). Ethnic minority research: Trends and directions. In E. E. Jones & S. J. Korchin (Eds.), *Minority mental health* (pp. 41-56). New York: Praeger.

Summit on spirituality. (1997, Spring). *ACES Spectrum,* pp. 14-15.

Szapocznik, J., Santisteban, D., Kurtines, W. M., Hervis, O. E., & Spencer, F. (1982). Life enhancements counseling: A psychosocial model of services for Cuban elders. In E. E. Jones & S. J. Korchin (Eds.), *Minority mental health* (pp. 296-329). New York: Praeger.

Thomas, A., & Sillen, S. (1972). *Racism and psychiatry.* New York: Brunner/Mazel

Thomas, C. W. (1971). *Boys no more.* Beverly Hills, CA: Glencoe.

Thomas, R. R. (1990, March/April). From affirmative action to affirming diversity. *Harvard Business Review,* pp. 107-117.

Thompson, C. E. (1995). Helms's White racial identity development (WRID) theory: Another look. *Counseling Psychologist, 22,* 645-649.

Thompson, L. A. (1989). *Romans and Blacks.* Norman: University of Oklahoma Press.

Toporek, R., & Reza, J. V. (1994, October). *Your professional development plan: Becoming cross culturally competent.* Paper presented at the Association for Multicultural Counseling and Development Western Summit III, San Diego, CA.

U.S. Bureau of the Census. (1992). *Statistical abstract of the United States. The national data book* (112th ed.). Washington, DC: Author.

Vega, W., & Murphy, J. W. (1990). *Culture and the restructuring of community mental health.* Westport, CT: Greenwood.

Vontress, C. E. (1971). Racial differences: Impediments to rapport. *Journal of Counseling Psychology, 18,* 7-13.

Weeks, W. H., Pedersen, P. B., & Brislin, R. W. (Eds.). (1977). *A manual of structured experiences for cross-cultural learning.* Yarmouth, ME: Intercultural Press.

Wehrly, B. (1995). *Pathways to multicultural counseling competence.* Pacific Grove, CA: Brooks/Cole.

Weinrach, S. G., & Thomas, K. R. (1996). The counseling profession's commitment to diversity-sensitive counseling: A critical reassessment. *Journal of Counseling and Development, 74,* 472-477.

White, J. L., & Parham, T. A. (1990). *The psychology of Blacks.* Englewood Cliffs, NJ: Prentice Hall.

Winter, S. (1977). Rooting out racism. *Issues in Radical Therapy, 17,* 24-30.

Wirth, L. (1945). The problem of minority groups. In R. Linton (Ed.), *The science of man in the world crisis* (pp. 347-372). New York: Columbia University Press.

Wrenn, C. G. (1962). The culturally encapsulated counselor. *Harvard Educational Review, 32,* 444-449.

Wrenn, C. G. (1985). Afterward: The culturally encapsulated counselor revisited. In P. B. Pedersen (Ed.), *Handbook of cross-cultural counseling and therapy* (pp. 323-329). Westport, CT: Greenwood.

Zitzow, D., & Estes, G. (1981). The heritage consistency continuum in counseling Native American children. In Spring Conference on Contemporary American Issues (Ed.), *American Indian issues in higher education* (pp. 133-139). Aberdeen, SD: ERIC Document Reproduction Service No. ED 209 305.

Zuckerman, M. (1990). Some dubious premises in research and theory on racial differences. *American Psychologist, 45,* 1297-1303.

Name Index

Subject Index

African Americans, 10, 24, 68-69, 95
   active therapeutic approach, 86
   culture, 7
   ethical codes, 85
   holistic outlook, 90
   spirituality/religion, 91
   See also Black racial identity; Black
     racial identity development models
Alternative helping roles, 87-89
American Business Association, 43
American Counseling Association (ACA),
   ix, 43, 83, 126
   cross-cultural competencies
     endorsement, xiii, 30, 129
   revised code of ethics, 84
American Psychological Association
   (APA), ix, 26, 43, 83, 126
   cross-cultural competencies
     endorsement, xiii, 30, 129
Antiracism training, 48
Anti-White, 32, 33
Asian American Identity development
   models:
   Kim Japanese American model, 72-73
   Kitano Japanese American model, 71-72
   limitations, 72

   stage process models, 72
   Sue and Sue Chinese American model, 71
Asian Americans/Pacific Islanders, 10, 95
   active therapeutic approach, 86
   culture, 7
   helping relationships, 85-86
Association for Counselor Education:
   spirituality competencies, 91-92
Association for Multicultural Counseling
   and Development, 28, 36
   Professional Standards Committee, 28

Bias:
   covert, 36
   unintentional, 36
Black racial identity, 69
Black racial identity development models,
   69-71, 76
   Cross model, 69-70

Civil Rights Act, 1964, 2, 23, 96
Civil rights movement, 2, 23, 24, 95
"Color blindness," 57

152

About the Authors

Robert T. Carter is Associate Professor of Psychology and Education, Program in Counseling Psychology, Teachers College, Columbia University, and Director of the Teachers College Winter Roundtable National Conference on Cross-Cultural Psychology and Education. He is known nationally and internationally for his work on Black racial identity and White racial identity, has published extensively in the areas of psychotherapy process and outcome, career development, cultural values, racial identity issues, educational achievement, and equity in education through the lens of racial identity. He has authored *The Influence of Race and Racial Identity in Psychotherapy: Toward a Racially Inclusive Model;* coedited, with Chalmer E. Thompson, *Racial Identity Theory: Applications for Individuals, Groups, and Organizations;* and is the editor of *Addressing Cultural Issues in Organizations.* In addition, he is the series editor for *Discussions From the Roundtable—The Counseling Psychologist*'s and the Roundtable Book series on multicultural psychology and education. He has done extensive consulting and training for many organizations, maintains a clinical practice, and serves on many editorial boards of scientific publications.

J. Manuel Casas received his Ph.D. from Stanford University with a specialization in the areas of counseling and cross-cultural psychology.

Currently, he is a professor in the counseling, clinical, and school psychology program at the University of California, Santa Barbara. Recognized nationally as one of the leading experts in the cross-cultural diversity areas of psychology, he has published widely and served on numerous editorial boards. He is the coauthor of the *Handbook of Racial/Ethnic Minority Counseling Research* and is one of the editors of the *Handbook of Multicultural Counseling*. His most recent research and publication endeavors have focused on Hispanic families and children who are at risk for experiencing educational and psycho-social problems, including drug and alcohol abuse. His research in this area gives special attention to the resiliency factors that can help Hispanic families avoid and/or overcome such problems. As president of JMC & Associates, one of the few Hispanic-owned diversity consulting and research companies, he serves as a consultant to various agencies and organizations.

Nadya A. Fouad is Associate Dean of the School of Education and a professor in the Department of Educational Psychology at the University of Wisconsin-Milwaukee. She received her Ph.D. in counseling psychology from the University of Minnesota in 1984. She has published numerous articles and chapters on cross-cultural vocational assessment, career development, interest measurement, and cross-cultural counseling. She is associate editor of the *Journal of Vocational Behavior* and coeditor of the new series, "Legacies and Traditions" in *The Counseling Psychologist*. She is a Fellow of Division 17 of the American Psychological Association, and is serving Division 17 as Vice President for Diversity and Public Interest, as well as chair-elect of the Society for Vocational Psychology, a Section of the Division.

Allen E. Ivey received his Ed.D. from Harvard University. He is currently Distinguished University Professor at the University of Massachusetts, Amherst. An ABPP in counseling psychology, he is a past president and Fellow of the Division of Counseling Psychology and a Fellow of the Society for the Psychological Study of Ethnic Minority Issues, Divisions 17 and 45 of the American Psychological Association. The originator of microcounseling and developmental counseling and therapy, he has won wide recognition and national and international awards including the American Counseling Association's Professional Development Award. Author or coauthor of over 25 books and 200 articles, his works have been translated into at least 13 languages. He did original work on the multicultural implications of the microskills in 1968-1974 and has been increasing his work in multicultural studies ever since. He is coauthor of *A Theory of Multicultural Counseling and Therapy*. His most recent writings have focused on psychotherapy as liberation, and he is an active member of the Mebon Kernow, the nationalist party of Kernow/Cornwall, Greater Britain.

Margaret Jensen received her bachelor's degree in political science from Stanford University and her master's of counseling from California State University, Hayward. She is coordinator of Career Counseling Resources for the SMART System, Shasta county's one-stop employment and training system. She is involved in a countywide effort to train all social service providers about the availability of electronic career development resources, and coordinates career development activities for over 40 SMART partner agencies. Her work experience is quite varied: Supervisor of the JTPA Youth Programs for the Shasta County Private Industry Council, community mental health social rehabilitation, vocational rehabilitation, and university student services. She has spent time working in Indonesia with Volunteers in Asia, teaching English as a foreign language on Sumatra and Java, and serving as field office coordinator for the VIA program. In addition, she has provided intercultural communication skills training for a number of San Francisco Bay area businesses and the Luce Scholars Program. Her unpublished graduate thesis, *Building Multicultural Competencies for Mental Health Organizations,* forms the basis for several of the chapters in this book.

Teresa LaFromboise is Associate Professor of Counseling Psychology and Chair of Native American Studies at Stanford University. In addition to her interest in the stress-related problems of American Indians, her research topics include interpersonal influence in multicultural counseling and prevention, and the impact of racial identity and bicultural effectiveness on adolescent mental health. She has evaluated the effectiveness of a culturally tailored life skills curriculum on American Indian high school students' knowledge, beliefs, and ability to intervene in suicidal situations. She is currently developing an instrument to assess the bicultural competence of American Indian adolescents. As an author or coauthor, her publications include *American Indian Life Skills Development Curriculum,* "Psychological Impact of Biculturalism: Evidence and Theory" in *Psychological Bulletin,* and "American Indian Women and Psychology" in H. Landrine (Ed.) *Bringing Culture Diversity to Feminist Psychology.* She is a past president of Division 45 of the American Psychological Association: Society for the Psychological Study of Ethnic Minority Issues.

Jeanne E. Manese is a counseling and consulting psychologist with Psychological and Counseling Services at the University of California, San Diego. In this capacity, she served as acting training director in their American Psychological Association-accredited predoctoral internship program. She is also the consulting psychologist to Thurgood Marshall College and Peer Counseling Program Coordinator. Her current research includes mental health issues with Asian student populations, multicultural competencies, and supervision. She is an active member of Divisions 17 (Counseling Psychology), 38 (Health Psychology), and 45 (Ethnic Minority Issues). She is a certified trainer of psychologists for the APA HIV Office for Psychology Education Program (HOPE) with an emphasis on the treatment of women and communities of color. She has been active in the Association of Counseling Center Training Agents and is a member of the Asian American Psychological Association. In addition to an active private practice, she provides consultation and training in various educational, medical, and corporate settings.

Ena Vazquez-Nuttall is director of the school psychology doctoral and 6th-year specialist program at Northeastern University in Boston. She is also associate dean and director of the graduate school of Bouve College of Pharmacy and Health Sciences. She practices privately conducting assessments of children, especially of Spanish-speaking backgrounds. She received a 5-year grant from the Merci Foundation to direct her students to conduct research on the impact of culture on emotional disturbance and retardation in children and families. She has published widely in the field of multicultural assessment and intervention, including revising a co-authored book titled *Assessing and Screening Preschoolers: Psychological and Educational Dimensions* to be published in 1998. She has received many awards from professional associations, including the National Association of School Psychologists, the American Counseling Association, the Massachusetts Psychological Association, and the Massachusetts Association of School Psychologists.

Joseph G. Ponterotto is Professor of Education in the Counseling and Counseling Psychology Programs at Fordham University-Lincoln Center. He received his Ph.D. in counseling psychology from the University of California at Santa Barbara. He is a Fellow of the American Psychological Association: (Divisions 17 and 45), and the American Association of Applied and Preventive Psychology. In 1994, he was the co-winner of APA Division 17's Early Career Scientist/Practitioner Award. He is coauthor or coeditor of five books and has published extensively in professional journals. A review in the July 1997, issue of *Contemporary Psychology* nominated the *Handbook of Multicultural Counseling* as a "contemporary classic," and the book is considered a "best seller" by Sage Publications. His 1993 book, *Preventing Prejudice* was named an "outstanding book" on the subject of human rights in North America by the Gustavus Myers Center for the Study of Human Rights. Presently, he is working on the second edition of the *Handbook of Racial/Ethnic Minority Counseling Research.*

Derald Wing Sue is Professor at the California School of Professional Psychology, Alameda and the California State University at Hayward. He was the cofounder and first president of the Asian American Psychological Association and is currently president-elect of the Society for the Psychological Study of Ethnic Minority Issues. An active member of the American Counseling Association and the American Psychological Association (Divisions 17 and 45), he is a Fellow of three Divisions of the latter (1, 17, 45), a Fellow of the American Psychological Society and the American Association of Applied and Preventive Psychology. He has published extensively in the field of multicultural counseling and therapy, and is the coauthor of three texts considered classics in the field: *Counseling the Culturally Different: Theory and Practice, Counseling American Minorities: A Cross-Cultural Perspective,* and *A Theory of Multicultural Counseling and Therapy.* In addition to an active national and international multicultural consulting practice with business, industry, government, mental health, and education, he is the producer of widely used videotapes on multiculturalism. He is the recipient of numerous awards from professional organizations, educational institutions, and community groups. He has chaired three major multicultural task force committees resulting in the development of multicultural counseling competencies—of which this book represents one of the products.

DATE DUE